PADDY
REILLY

TOM GILMORE has worked as a journalist and broadcaster for over forty years. He has been a staff reporter with the *Tuam Herald* for most of this time, as well as a freelance contributor to most Irish national newspapers.

He has worked with Galway Bay FM for thirty years, as a newsreader-reporter and a presenter of country music programmes.

Tom is the author of *Big Tom: The King of Irish Country* and *Paddy Cole: King of the Swingers* for O'Brien Press. His first book was *Larry Cunningham: A Showband Legend* in 2009, and he contributed the Irish chapter to *The Blackwell Guide to Recorded Country Music*.

Tom is a native of Bodane, Tuam, County Galway.

PADDY REILLY

From The Fields Of Athenry to The Dubliners And Beyond

**Paddy Reilly with
Tom Gilmore**

THE O'BRIEN PRESS
DUBLIN

First published 2022 by The O'Brien Press Ltd,
12 Terenure Road East, Rathgar, Dublin 6, D06 HD27, Ireland.
Tel: +353 1 4923333; Fax: +353 1 4922777
E-mail: books@obrien.ie. Website: obrien.ie
The O'Brien Press is a member of Publishing Ireland.

ISBN: 978-1-78849-368-0

Book and cover design by Emma Byrne.

8 7 6 5 4 3 2 1
26 25 24 23 22

Printed and bound by ScandBook in the EU.
The paper in this book is produced using pulp from managed forests.

Picture credits: O'Reilly family: pages 10, 21, 43, 47, 48, 78, 81 and 146; Tom Lawlor: page 30 (both);
David Cleary: page 110; Colm Henry: page 127; Maxwell Photography: page 141.

Published in

Contents

Chapter I

Good Old Days My Arse!

In the war-torn world of 1939, Pat (Paddy) Reilly was born in the south Dublin village of Rathcoole. You might expect those early, formative years in Rathcoole to be viewed through rose-tinted glasses, as the good old days. 'Good old days my arse!' retorts the outspoken, internationally famous folk singer. Paddy loves his native Rathcoole, and always has. He kept a house there even during lengthy periods of living in America, and he still lives in the village. But he quickly dispels any notion that life, even in an idyllic village like Rathcoole, was a bed of roses back in the good old days when times were bad!

His rendition of the Pete St John song 'The Fields of Athenry' has become internationally famous. But it was fields near the opposite side of Ireland, far from Athenry, that helped form the character of the then Pat (later Paddy) Reilly.

Ireland's best-loved solo balladeer, as well as being a member of The Dubliners, Paddy is an unassuming man who can turn any conversation into an erudite discussion. Having left school at thirteen, he was educated in the 'university of life'. But his penchant for reading books, on topics from world politics to philosophy, sport and music, makes him a well-versed conversationalist on diverse subjects.

He is also revered and respected by his fans and peers in the music business for many other hits, including 'The Town I Loved So Well', 'Flight of the Earls', 'Spancil Hill', 'Dublin Saunter' and 'The Craic Was Ninety In the Isle of Man'.

Not only did Paddy gain respect as an entertainer from international political and sporting personalities, but many of them became personal friends of his as well. Close friends included the late Senator Edward Kennedy and Speaker Tip O'Neill in American politics. In international sporting circles, Paddy befriended Jack Charlton, George Best, Johnny Giles, Ray Treacy, Pat Jennings, Liam Brady, Frank Stapleton and snooker ace Alex Higgins. He has plenty of funny tales to tell about nights out with them, especially around Manchester and Birmingham.

Of course, his biggest heroes of all are members of his beloved Dublin football teams. These include the recent six-in-a-row Dubs team of the past decade, along with earlier trainers and players from the 1950s and '60s, including his contemporary Kevin 'Heffo' Heffernan.

Paddy smiles when he recalls his friend from the Irish music scene, the late Larry Cunningham, jokingly calling him 'the Dublin culchie'.

'I never liked the term "culchie", as I regard it as derogatory to country people when city folk use it. But because Larry was from the country, and proud of it, we often had a laugh when he called me that,' he says.

Growing up, either in Dublin or in the country, going to school and finding work in the hungry '40s and '50s wasn't easy. Life could be harsh, even in a scenic south Dublin village such as Rathcoole, where Paddy and his sisters Jean and Linda were raised.

'I don't believe in the good old days. They were dreadful days for a lot of people. However, I wouldn't change them now. We had nothing, but we didn't know we had nothing, because nobody had anything,' he says.

Even if the Reillys didn't have much, like most people in the 1940s, music was a constant in their home. But it wasn't always folk or trad music – Paddy also had a penchant for opera from an early age.

'My father brought me to an opera when I was very young. The Dublin Grand Opera Society were in the Olympia Theatre. I remember we were in "the gods", and it reminded me when I brought my son Ciarán to the Metropolitan Opera House in New York when he was a child. I went to see a Wagner play in the gods in the Olympia for two shillings with my father, and I thought I'd hate it, but Jesus, I liked it; I loved it.

'I remember going to see Louise Dudley singing *The Merry Widow* in the Gaiety, which was beautiful. I was sold on opera and operetta after that. I went to see Franz Lehar's *The Merry Widow*, which was an operetta, but it was made into a fully-fledged opera in the Metropolitan Opera House in 1984, and I was there. I was thrilled because it had a major influence on my interest in that type of music,' says Paddy.

In an interview with Kay Doyle in *Ireland's Own* magazine in 2019, Paddy recalled again going to the opera after visiting his mother in hospital.

The Reilly family, 1956 (left to right): Paddy, his mother Ellen, sisters Jean and Linda and his father Jack.

'The Dublin Grand Opera Festival was on, and my mother was in St Patrick Dun's Hospital at the same time. My father gave me half a crown (two shillings and six pence in "old" money) to see her. I hitchhiked into town to save the bus fare that Dad had given me, and I went to the opera after visiting my mother in hospital.'

During his childhood days in Rathcoole, his sister Linda also brought him to the cinema, though he had less interest in that. 'Linda was very sophisticated; she was a bit sophisticated for Rathcoole, but sadly she died very young, at twenty-five. As a child, she would bring me to the pictures to see *The Pickwick Papers* and *Little Women*, classics like that. I didn't have much interest in them, but I was brought anyway to introduce me to Charles Dickens,' says Paddy with a laugh.

Paddy did a bit of acting himself at a youthful age with a local group, and he won an All-Ireland award for it. The late Anna Manahan was the adjudicator when Paddy won his gold medal for acting. She later won a Tony award in the USA for her part in the play *The Beauty Queen of Leenane*. Paddy smiles as he recalls winning his gold medal:

'Yeah, I won an All-Ireland medal in Athlone, but not for football! It was with the Rathcoole Players. The Rathcoole Dramatic Society used to practice in the library here in the village. Anna Manahan awarded me the gold medal for our production of *Drama at Inish*, written by Lennox Robinson.'

At an early age, Paddy was working on the farm and at the stables of the nearby Taaffe family, famous in horse racing circles. It was tough work for the youngster, but he has happy memories of it too.

'Well, everybody worked. I worked on all the farms, doing little bits. I was never a permanent member of the staff at Taaffe's, but I worked in the yard. I worked for all the farmers around, picking turnips and potatoes and picking stones. I remember picking stones on Taaffe's gallops. I've never seen so many fucking stones in my whole life,' laughs Paddy.

While Irish rebel songs are among those that Paddy sings, they have never been the fulcrum of his live programme or of his recordings. They are only a part of his vast repertoire of folk songs. But he could hardly miss hearing such songs growing up as the son of a man who fought in the Irish War of Independence and the Civil War.

The divisions in Ireland that emanated from the country's bitter Civil War continued to manifest themselves even when Paddy was a youngster in the '40s and '50s. Rural Rathcoole was, unfortunately, like so many other Irish villages, inhabited by people still divided against each other, due to their different sides in the Civil War.

There was a slight age gap between Paddy's parents, Jack and Nellie Reilly, when they got married. But that was not unusual in the 1920s.

'They were married very young,' says Paddy. 'My father was on the run during the Civil War up in the Wicklow Mountains, but I'm not sure what year they married. I think my mother was nineteen and my father was six years older.'

Their home in Rathcoole was one of three houses close together on their part of the street. Following the Civil War, the heads of the three households were of different political persuasions. It didn't always lead to harmonious neighbourly relations, especially around election times, as Paddy recalls.

'The three houses on the street were Attleys, Timmons and Reillys. The three men were total opposites in their political views. My father was Fianna Fáil, Kit Timmons was a Blueshirt (Fine Gael) and Kit Attley was a staunch Labour Party man. How they kept a lid on their differences and remained friends I'll never know. They used to put up posters for their respective parties at election times outside their doors. One would be putting them up and the other pulling them down,' he laughs.

Paddy's best friend growing up was his next-door neighbour Bill Attley. He later became a well-known trade unionist and Labour party activist, and was the first joint president of SIPTU. Bill was best man at Paddy's wedding, and Paddy was best man at Bill's wedding. They are still firm friends, and Paddy's daughter Ashling is married to Bill's son Colin.

While the Labour party were neutral in the tragic Irish Civil War that followed the War of Independence, there was a terrible bitterness between the two main political parties. On one side were the Free Staters, led by Michael Collins, who became Cumann Na nGaedheal and later Fine Gael.

They favoured working within the Irish peace treaty brokered with the British. The opposition, often known as the Irregulars or Sinn Féin, was led by Éamon de Valera. Most of his followers later mutated into Fianna Fáil, while others remained as Sinn Féin. The bitterness between the Collins camp and de Valera's crew was palpable, and it remained and manifested itself regularly in Rathcoole when Paddy was growing up and afterwards.

'Oh, my father would have been very bitter. There were a lot of people living in Rathcoole who professed to be republican supporters, but they weren't. My father was the real thing. He was there through the thick of it all; he was on the run after the Civil War,' says Paddy.

Their neighbour Kit Timmons became more affluent when he got a job as an overseer with Dublin County Council. So being part of the Free State side may have had its benefits – or maybe not!

However, while Paddy's father didn't support his neighbours' political views, he was not too proud to wear his shoes and clothes, given to him after Mr Timmons died. 'Yes, Kit Timmons was a bit more affluent, and he had suits and all that, and my father got those and his shoes when he passed away. We were going to Croke Park one day and the shoes were hurting him, and I said, "Are you all right, Dad?"

'My father replied, "These shoes are hurting me." I said, "Jesus, don't tell me you bought shoes that are too small for your feet."

'He retorted, "They're not my shoes; they're Kit Timmons's shoes, and he never bought anything right in his life." What could I do but laugh?' recalls Paddy.

Going to Croke Park with his father for football matches was a regular occurrence for Paddy Reilly, even on days when his dad didn't want him there. 'My father brought me to Croke Park every Sunday. He went there each Sunday, no matter who was playing. On big days, I used to have to hide on the bus – he wouldn't bring me, because it was too crowded, especially on St Patrick's Day for the Railway Cup matches, which were big back then. I would get on the bus and hide until it had passed through Saggart village. Then I would come up and sit beside him and he was stuck with me!

'We were on the canal end of the stadium, and I was on my father's shoulders, when Mayo won one of their two-in-a-row All-Irelands. It was either 1950 or '51, and I remember in particular the "flying doctor", Pádraig Carney, who was one of the Mayo stars. He later emigrated to work as a doctor in New York, but they flew him home to play for Mayo again in two other vital matches. It was a gruelling twenty-hour flight in those days in a bumpy Viscount (turbo prop) plane. But he was obviously vital for them winning All-Ireland and National League titles.'

According to the *Mayo Advertiser* on 28 February 2020, 'The Mayo County Board brought him back from New York for the Mayo vs Dublin National League semi-final on 25 April 1954 (he had emigrated in March), and he captained Mayo to a thrilling 0-11 to 0-7 victory over the favourites, Dublin. Micheál Ó Hehir, the legendary GAA commentator, immortalised Pádraig that day as "The Flying Doctor". He was brought back again for the League final, in which he led Mayo to a decisive victory over Carlow. This was his last competitive game on Irish soil.'

Paddy Reilly's interest in Gaelic football increased as the 1950s progressed, and that sporting interest was nurtured in no small way by the success of the great Dublin teams towards the end of that decade. Paddy's father remained a loyal Dublin fan, but he wasn't too enamoured by the number of players from St Vincent's club on the 1955 team.

'My father wouldn't have liked Vincent's all that much, because they were always beating St Marys. But in 1955, when Kerry beat Dublin, they were all Vincent's players except for the goalkeeper.'

While the final score of Kerry 0-12 to Dublin's 1-6 suggests that it was a close encounter, Paddy has different memories of it: 'Kerry kicked the shit out of Dublin. Kevin Heffernan never forgot it, and he never got over it until his dying day. He never got over Kerry beating Dublin in 1955, ever.'

Away from the sports fields, Paddy worked in the fields around Rathcoole, often with horses, as the village is near Ireland's most famous county for raising racehorses, Kildare. 'Sure, almost everyone around here, especially in Kildare and South County Dublin, has a horse,' he says with a grin.

Travelling for hours on the crossbar of his father's bike to go cutting turf in the mountains is another abiding memory. Jack Reilly would cycle thirty-two kilometres, with young Paddy on the crossbar of the bike and a sleán for cutting turf strapped underneath, to cut turf on Kippure Mountain near Wicklow.

'After such a long, hard cycle, mostly uphill for hours, he still had to do a tough day's work on the bog, cutting the turf. Then he had to cycle home in the evenings, again with me on the bar of the bike. He packed two days' work into one.

'All we had was a bit of bread, tea, sugar, milk in a bag and a billycan. In that we would boil water over a turf fire for our lunch break from that back-breaking work,' says Paddy. Paddy helped from an early age with the 'footing' of the turf, and then 'clamping' it into bigger heaps. When dry, the turf was filled, again by hand, into a lorry to take it home.

At home, along with his siblings Jean and Linda, they often listened to their mother singing old Irish ballads. Nellie sang sometimes at house parties in the locality, and sometimes Jack might sing or just hum along. Those parties were popular in country areas at that time, before bigger halls and bands came along.

'We were considered by city folk to be living in the country. People from Dublin used to come out to Rathcoole to pick blackberries, and they thought we lived in the bush, which we did. There was nothing much here. Three pubs in Rathcoole and that was it.'

Nowadays, Rathcoole is not so rural – it's a busy, prosperous suburb of south Dublin. But the Rathcoole of Paddy's childhood was far removed from the affluent place it is today. In the 1940s, like so many other urban and rural areas, it was ravaged by tuberculosis (TB). In those days, if you were not so lucky, you might find yourself having to go for treatment for TB to Peamount Sanatorium. Paddy and his sisters Jean and Linda were luckier than some of their friends, as they never contracted the disease, which for many people was fatal.

'TB was rampant. Almost every youngster got TB, sometimes from milk. I used to deliver milk to three or four houses every morning before I went to school. I used to go down College Lane to Cullen's Yard, and got the milk straight from the cow's spin. It was never pasteurised, and many of the cattle had TB.

'Luckily, we never had TB in our house. Now, when I think back on it, my mother was never outside of Rathcoole in her life, but she was a very bright person. She wouldn't let me join the pipe band in Rathcoole, until eventually I agreed to play the drums. Only then did she let me join the band. She wouldn't let me go blowing a chanter, in case I got TB off it. Everybody thought she was crazy, but she was right. My parents were both musicians, but very anti-drink, and they wouldn't be very permissive about us going to pubs when I was growing up,' he says.

Of all the friends he went to school with, Paddy says that, sadly, he remembers many getting TB and others emigrating. But he laughs aloud when he says that he 'didn't stay at school very long anyway'!

'Oh! The little schooling that I got wasn't a lot, as I left school at thirteen anyway. But most of the lads who were in my class also left school at an early age. Very often, a day or two after they finished school, they took the boat to England to try to find work. Of course, many came home again, but often it was only for family funerals.

'I remember a great friend of mine, Pat Timmons, coming home for his mother's funeral at a time when Dublin were playing Clare at Croker (Croke Park). It was sensational that Clare were in the Championship, and I suggested to him that he should not go back on Saturday, but stay for the match on Sunday.

'But he said, "Ah, we'd never get tickets." I said that I could get tickets if he stayed, and he did.'

When Paddy and Pat Timmons were in the Hogan Stand bar, Pat said they should probably get out of there before there was any trouble. He was worried, because the two groups of fans were drinking and in full song in the same pub. Paddy had to tell him that it wasn't like the football matches in England, where there would be trouble at games between rival supporters. 'There was never any of that at any of the GAA games. Sure, we were all from the same country anyway,' laughs Paddy.

'I worked in Taaffe's farm before I got my first regular job, in a local petrol filling station,' recalls Paddy. 'I have many memories of both jobs, including about Ben Hannon, who used to drive a tractor at Taaffe's farm; he went on to become a famous jockey. He ended up riding a horse in America during a dispute at the stables. One of the others was supposed to go to the US with the horse. But when a dispute arose, it wasn't any of them that went. Another lad who worked in the yard got the job of going to America with the horse when the stable lads went on strike. Ben Hannon was brought in from driving the tractor to help muck out from the horses.

'He ended up riding that horse, even though he had never rode before, and he became a very famous jockey. He rode two Cheltenham Festival winners, including the Two-Mile Champion Chase on a horse named Muir. Ben also won the Honeybourne Novices' Chase in Cheltenham, a year before the famous horse Arkle won it.'

Tom Taaffe had an 'eye' for picking a winning horse for training. When he saw Mr What in a field near Mullingar, coming home for racing in Roscommon, he suspected the animal was going to be a winner. That's according to Anne Holland in her book *The Grand National: The Irish at Aintree*:

'Tom bought the horse to be called Mr What – because nobody could think of a name for him – for £500 from its breeder Mrs Barbra O'Neill. His choice was testament to his good "eye", for several English trainers had already turned him down.

'Most pundits still considered Mr What too much of a novice for Aintree. This is where the Aintree factor comes in: Mr What thrived on the challenge.'

Paddy recalls mixed emotions in the Taaffe stable regarding the sensational success of Mr What in the 1958 Grand National. 'It was kind of a happy and sad relationship really, because Tos Taaffe was working in the yard with his father, but he didn't ride the horse. Pat Taaffe was first jockey to Tom Draper, and Tos Taaffe was first jockey to Vincent O'Brien. O'Brien had a horse that was something of a semi-favourite for the Grand

National, and the horse was declared to run in the race. But Ted Walsh (jockey, racehorse trainer and commentator) told me one day at the races that he suspects O'Brien knew the horse wasn't going to run. However, he still declared the horse, until there was nobody around to ride Mr What. They were still hoping that Tos might get the ride. But as Vincent O'Brien, where Tos worked, kept declaring the other horse until the last minute, it was sad that Tos wasn't riding the winning horse.'

Mr What was ridden by Arthur Freeman, and won by thirty lengths. As Paddy worked part-time in Taaffe's yard, he got the honour of walking the Grand National winner through the streets of Rathcoole. Back in 1958, that was like rock star stuff!

Paddy vividly remembers that moment of fame in his native village in 1958. So perhaps there were some good old days (and nights) in Rathcoole after all? 'Oh! Jesus, the celebrations went on for a week. The pubs were open twenty-four hours a day. It was an exciting time,' laughs Paddy. Paddy, proud as punch, leading the winning horse through the village, was immortalised in a photograph that hung in the local Poitín Stil pub.

Around that time, the young Pat (later Paddy) Reilly got his first 'regular' job, at a local petrol station. 'Yeah, Mrs Fitzgerald owned the local petrol station and the first job I ever had was working for her. The sandmen in their lorries, mostly boys from Kill, Co. Kildare, used to get their fuel there. I used to have to pass the fuel hose between the cabin and the truck, but one day, I left the hose stuck in the truck. I was the first man to discover oil in Rathcoole!' he roars.

'I went away to write out the receipt for the driver and gave it to him, and left the hose still in the pipe leading to the tank of the truck. He drove off and pulled the fuel pump down. There was fuel blasting up towards the sky. It was like a geyser. The poor woman who owned the filling station was a bad asthmatic, and that incident nearly caused her to die from an asthmatic attack.'

In those days, if a stranger, or anyone of note, passed through the village, the locals took notice. Paddy vividly remembers the actor Noel Purcell travelling through in his Mark 2 Jaguar motor on his way to the races at The Curragh or Naas. Noel Purcell sometimes stopped at the Rathcoole filling station for petrol.

'Even when not working at the filling station, I would sometimes just sit on the bridge waiting for Noel Purcell's Jaguar to go by. It was a sensational-looking vehicle in the 1960s. I think it was one of the first of that model they manufactured, maybe around 1958 or 1960.

'Noel was a gentleman and a real Dub. I remember he had the first transistor radio I ever saw. It was one day at the races in Naas, and I was walking around with him, just to be close to him. Then another little young fella came up to him and shouted, "Mr Purcell, Mr Purcell! What's the score?" as Noel was listening to the match from Lansdowne Road. Noel replied, "It's eight to six now." "But for who, Mr Purcell?" shouted the youth. "Oh! It's eight for Ireland, ya little bollix ya," Noel replied as he roared out laughing.'

Paddy only got to know Noel Purcell 'very fleetingly', as he was an old man even at that time and already a Hollywood star. But he says that Purcell stood out in a crowd and had great gravitas.

'My memory of Noel is that he was huge man – he was like six-foot-three, which back then we thought made him look like a monster. King Henry VII was five-foot-six, or something like that, and he was considered a big man. But Purcell was also very, very striking. He would walk into a room and everyone would stop and stare. And, like Sean Connery, he had a great speaking voice. He got all these characters parts, usually as a pirate or whatever. But a nice man. He liked his horses, and he liked the racing.'

In the early 1960s, Pat Reilly moved on to a job in the nearby Saggart Paper Mills. 'I was working shift work, which, to put it mildly, I didn't like very much. While I didn't dislike my job, I hated the shift work,' he says.

He was following in his father's footsteps by working in the paper mills, as Jack Reilly had worked in the Swiftbrook Paper Mills, which was the main local employer. It had a famous connection with the Irish Rebellion of 1916, as the paper used for printing 'The Proclamation of the Irish Republic' came from there.

His parents were happy that he was in what they regarded as a permanent, pensionable job. But for Paddy, one of the big plusses was that it

Paddy in his back garden, 1960.

provided money to purchase a car. However, at that time, petrol was costly. To save enough money for petrol to drive to see his favourite music group, The Dubliners, at weekends, Paddy had to walk to work during the week!

'The Dubliners used to play in Howth every Saturday night. It was the Dubs when the group was in its infancy, and they were brilliant. But during the week I would walk to work. I would get up at 5am to walk to work for 6am, to have enough money for petrol to go to Howth on the Saturday nights to see those Dubliners. Good old days my bollix!' he roars.

It was during those days that Paddy first became friends with the members of the group. It is a friendship that lasted during their lifetimes. In those far-flung days, as a young fan of the famous folk group, he never dreamed that decades later, he too would be one of The Dubliners.

'I became friends with them at those gigs in Howth, especially with Luke Kelly. He was going back and forth at the time to Birmingham, where he lived sometimes. He only came home the odd weekend.

'Luke was selling communist newspapers in Birmingham, and he wasn't at home in Dublin that much. It was just when they started doing the Royal Hotel in Howth that Luke used to come home more often at weekends to join them. Then he moved home permanently. He didn't have a chance of going to America – Luke had trouble getting in, because he was a registered communist!' laughs Paddy.

When it is suggested to him that Luke may have been a socialist activist rather than a communist, Paddy emits another loud guffaw of laughter. 'He was the only communist I knew who ever lived in the Victorian area of Dublin known as Dartmouth Square!'

Before he was 'discovered' as a singer of note (pardon the pun!) at The Embankment in Tallaght, Paddy's earlier exploits singing in pubs 'for the craic' influenced him to buy a guitar at the age of twenty-five. He purchased it from an advertisement in a newspaper. He described that transaction in a 2019 interview with Kay Doyle in *Ireland's Own*:

'There was a lad on the North Circular Road selling a pair of football boots and a guitar for thirty bob (£1.50). I went in and picked them up. I still have the guitar; it was a piece of junk, and I gave the boots to the first kid I met on the street.'

Initially, Paddy was only singing in bars, such as O'Donoghue's, often just for the fun of it and sometimes after a few pints! 'Well, I also went to O'Donoghue's pub around the same time The Dubliners were taking off, when I used to drive to Howth to hear them. I had been going to O'Donoghue's pub for years, because there was music regularly in that pub. There was always someone singing or playing the whistle or some other instrument.'

Strangely enough, the first song that Ireland's favourite ballad singer learned on his guitar wasn't a ballad at all. It was a pop hit from the 1960s by UK singer Donovan, titled 'Yellow is the Colour'.

Paddy is brutally frank about his guitar playing. 'If I were hanged for being a musician, I'd be hanged in total innocence. I could sing, and I also played the guitar. In fact, I toured the world playing the guitar knowing only three chords,' he roars.

But one of Ireland's most respected guitarists, former member of The Dubliners Eamon Campbell, often said that Paddy was one of the best guitarists, in the fingerpicking style, that he had known.

Chapter 2

From Pat to Paddy Reilly

When Paddy was starting to play in pubs such as O'Donoghue's in Dublin, the ballad revival was only starting in Ireland. Back then, he was known as Pat Reilly and not Paddy. The Dubliners were at the forefront of the ballad boom here, but in America, The Clancy Brothers and Tommy Makem had started a sensational interest in Irish folk music a few years earlier.

'I kinda started as the ballad boom was gaining momentum here, and you could say that I was part of the ballad boom. I came in with the tide, you know,' laughs Paddy. 'Two groups started it all on either side of the Atlantic. The Clancy Brothers made it in America and the Dubliners made it in Ireland. Then we all came after that; anybody who says they weren't influenced by the Clancys or the Dubliners is a liar.

'No Dubliners or no Clancys, and there would have been no revival. The Clancys started the Folk bug in America, in The Lion's Head in Greenwich Village. Then the Dubliners started it here and in England. If The Dubliners hadn't done so, I think the ballad scene would have been slower to take off here. They were unique.'

In America, The Clancy Brothers and Tommy Makem lit the spark in 1956 that spread into a folk music flame. The Irish group became a phenomenon there throughout the 1960s. An album they first recorded with very little instrumentation at Columbia University in New York spawned their recording success. At that time, brothers Paddy and Tom Clancy were training as actors in New York, and the recently arrived emigrants Liam Clancy and Tommy Makem had very little singing experience.

But the reaction to that formative recording by the group was good enough for them to re-record the same album of Irish rebel songs, this time with instrumentation, in 1958. After that, their albums reflected more of the craic, and the lighter side of Irish life and music, rather than emphasising rebel songs.

So successful were The Clancy Brothers and Tommy Makem that in 1961, they were a hit on the prestigious 'Ed Sullivan Show' on US television. The following year, they entertained President John F Kennedy and his wife Jackie and their guests on St Patrick's Day in the White House.

One could say that The Clancy Brothers and Tommy Makem re-introduced Irish music to the new world. Back home, in the old world of Ireland, the UK and Europe, The Dubliners were about to do likewise. The work of the two groups complemented each other.

When the Clancy Brothers and Tommy Makem returned in triumph to Dublin in 1963, music critics compared them to The Beatles. Paddy Reilly's girlfriend back then was among the youngsters screaming for The Clancy Brothers and Tommy Makem when they played in Dublin.

'I remember the first time the Clancys came to play in the National Stadium in Dublin. How could I ever forget it, as I was going out with a girl from Ballyfermot, and she queued overnight to get tickets for them? But that was a long time ago when we were very young, and I was still working in the paper mills.'

It seems that The Clancys and some members of The Dubliners exchanged songs and ideas when the brothers and Tommy Makem first played in Dublin. That is according to a story in *The Swingin' Sixties Book*, edited by the late John Coughlan, the man in charge of *Spotlight* pop magazine during that era:

'When The Clancys came to Dublin they stayed in suites in the Shelbourne and Ronnie, Barney, Luke and Ciarán paid fraternal visits. There was first class hospitality and exchange of professional ideas. Liam Clancy in particular was always keen to collect new material.'

Before Paddy started playing and singing himself, and during his nights off from gigging, he would go along to see acts from other music genres perform around Dublin.

'Long before I started gigging, as a youngster, I was going to The Pavilion in Saggart to the four-penny hops. These events took place there every Tuesday and Thursday night. It was a type of community centre, where people played records and we went to dance. It was the only place that boy could meet girl at that time,' he says.

Later, he would see many of the big stars in The Royal, 'now long pulled down', as it says in another Pete St John song, 'Dublin in the Rare Old Times'.

'I was there the night it closed down, and I never saw so many tears in my life. Everybody there was in floods of tears that night. Among those I saw there during my youth was Roy Rogers the singing cowboy, and his horse Trigger. In fact, Trigger was the big star on the night that I saw them at the Royal,' laughs Paddy.

Paddy continued working by day, and sometimes playing music part-time by night, and he has many happy memories of Dublin in those rare old times. Possibly one of the strangest memories was seeing the head of Admiral Horatio Nelson up on stage at a Dubliners gig!

'The Dubliners put on a special show in the Olympia Theatre. It was a play, featuring songs and drama by The Dubliners, and it attracted such huge crowds for Ronnie and the boys that you couldn't get into it. This was around the time that Nelson's Pillar was blown up. One night, during the middle of the show, Nelson's head appeared on stage! I can clearly remember the reaction in the aftermath of it – there was bloody murder about it,' laughs Paddy.

Nelson's Pillar, built in memory of the Vice-Admiral who defeated Napoleon at the Battle of Waterloo, was a landmark in Dublin for 157 years, until it was blown up. The blast occurred in the early hours of 8 March 1966. It was believed to be the work of a 'subversive group', according to news stories at the time, but nobody was ever charged with the blast.

'Those who blew up Nelson's Pillar knew what they were doing, but when the Irish Army had to blow up the stump afterwards, they nearly blew up half of the centre of Dublin,' laughs Paddy.

In an interview on RTÉ TV afterwards, Ronnie Drew said that the lads who brought Nelson's head to their gig left it on the stage in a big sack. "The audience asked was it the real thing or not, and Luke (Kelly) gave it a kick and it didn't fall over. Then they believed it was the real thing," said Ronnie.

According to the Irish Central website, 'Seven hearty students from the National College of Art and Design reportedly stole it from a storage shed in Clanbrassil Street. Later they leased it for over $300 a month to an antique dealer in London for his shop window.'

But in an interview on RTÉ TV at the time, the students' (hooded) spokesperson said they only took it to raise money for debts at the college. Today, the stone head rests in Pearse Street Library in Dublin.

Not everybody was pleased about the blowing up of the pillar. Senator David Norris, speaking on the RTÉ TV programme 'Fiorasach' in 2010, said, 'It was an ignorant thing to do.' He described the pillar as 'one of the iconic representations of Dublin'.

Record buyers at the time clearly enjoyed singing about the blowing up of the pillar though – a song 'Up Went Nelson' became a number-one hit for eight weeks. It was by a group of four Belfast teachers, who called themselves The Go Lucky Four. The Dubliners also reached number six in the same charts around the same time with 'Nelson's Farewell', written by Galway man Joe Dolan.

While Paddy got to know The Dubliners and The Clancys and their songs, he had greater difficulty hearing The Beatles sing when they played in Dublin. In November 1963, the Fab Four from Liverpool played two concerts at the Adelphi Cinema in Middle Abbey Street, and Paddy was there.

'While I saw The Beatles at a distance, I didn't hear a word of any of the songs they sang, because of all the screaming of the crowd. I never saw such hysteria in my life, with young girls screaming everywhere and hundreds of Gardaí trying to control the crowd. It ended up in a riot, with a lot of young people arrested,' he says.

Paddy's memories are corroborated by the front page of the *Irish Times* on the morning after the night before! 'Many arrested as city crowds riot' was the headline in bold type on the front page on 8 November 1963. The story said, 'More than a dozen youths were arrested and taken to various Garda stations last night when fights broke out as the Liverpool beat singers were playing at The Adelphi Cinema … Thousands gathered in the city centre and traffic was brought to a standstill as more than 200 Gardaí and 20 squad cars attempted to bring the situation under control.'

The story was accompanied by a photograph of a crowd of young people breaking through a police cordon on O'Connell Street, with others climbing on telephone kiosks. At least fifty people were reportedly injured in the melee, and three were taken to hospital.

There were no such scenes of fan hysteria when Paddy was singing in pubs around Dublin at that time! But he came to the attention of two music promoters, who saw star potential in him.

'I started doing gigs around Dublin, such as at Slattery's in Capel Street. Ah, there were several places in Dublin that I used to play; all of us on the ballad circuit used to the play the same ones.

'Then a fella called Eddie Storey, from the Irish Transport and General Workers Union, started doing concerts in Liberty Hall. It would have been my first experience of playing in a theatre setting when I played there. I was top of the bill there every other week, and it was a wonderful experience for me, doing that type of gig,' says Paddy.

When he started singing at The Embankment in Tallaght, he changed his name from Pat to Paddy Reilly.

'Mick McCarthy bought the Embankment, which was in the middle of nowhere. He said it was in Tallaght, to try to entice people to come.

Above: Mick McCarthy in The Embankment, 1974.
Below: Paddy Reilly & Luke Kelly onstage at The Embankment, 1974.

It's really in Saggart, but he thought Tallaght sounded closer to the city.

'He started bringing all the ballad groups to The Embankment. The Dubliners often played there on Monday nights, and I used to go up and sing in the bar every weekend. I was still on shift work at the paper mills, which I hated with a passion. But I would regularly head for The Embankment after finishing work at ten o'clock on Saturday nights.'

Paddy would sing in the bar there, just for the fun of it, and he says he always thought he sounded better after a pint or two!

'McCarthy heard me singing in the bar, and he was very direct in the way he said that I should be on the bigger stage, where they were paying to see acts perform. "You have it, you have it, you Dublin whore ya! You are better than all of them in there," McCarthy would say. That was after I had bought the second-hand guitar and learned to play it as well as I could.

'Mick convinced me to go into the lounge at The Embankment as a singer. I ended up singing for a fee, and when I was making more money from singing than from working in the paper mill, I ran like a rabbit from the shift work,' laughs Paddy.

'Mick McCarthy changed my name from Pat Reilly to Paddy Reilly. If there was no Mick McCarthy, I would never have been known as Paddy Reilly.'

During his stint playing at The Embankment, Paddy also made his first recordings. He says that he never heard the first LP that he was on, but he was one of four people singing on the album.

The album was called *The Gatecrashers*, and it featured songs by Danny Doyle, Shay Healy, Pecker Dunne and Paddy Reilly. Shay Healy sang his own song, 'Dollymount Strand', which would later become much more associated with Paddy. Paddy sang 'Pharaoh's Daughter', 'Well Fed Man' and 'Louse House in Kilkenny'.

'Yes, I was on it, and some other unbelievable people played, or sang, on it too. As far as I can remember, they included Tinkler Hassett, the Pecker Dunne and members of Emmet Spiceland. But they might have been named something else at that time.

'Danny Doyle sang most of the songs, and I think Johnny McEvoy might also have been on it. Johnny McEvoy used to play at The Embankment with a fella called Mick Crotty.'

Paddy says that the first record that he made on his own was 'The Curragh of Kildare'. 'I never became a very good guitar player, but I was so bad at playing the guitar back then that I wouldn't play it on the recording. Danny Doyle accompanied me singing on "The Curragh of Kildare". Poor Danny died last year in the USA,' he says.

Danny Doyle became a big star the year that *The Gatecrashers* album was released. But his big hit didn't come from the album. He had his first number one in the Irish pop charts with 'Whiskey On a Sunday' in late 1967. Earlier that year, he had two other top-ten hits in Ireland, with 'Step It Out Mary' and 'The Irish Soldier Laddie'.

Perhaps because of his growing popularity back in 1967, Danny was very much to the fore in the photograph on the sleeve of *The Gatecrashers*. In the picture, Shay Healy is playing a fiddle and Pecker Dunne is on the banjo. While Paddy is named on the front cover, and he sings three songs on the album, he is not pictured on the sleeve.

Later, when Paddy's debut solo album was released, when he had become much better known, his hallmark version of Shay's 'Dollymount Strand' became one of his most played tracks on radio.

Before emigrating to America, Danny Doyle, who played guitar on Paddy's first recording was, ironically, also the first to have a chart entry in

Ireland with 'The Fields of Athenry'. He had many more songs in the Irish pop charts, including 'Daisy a Day' and 'The Rare Old Times', during the late 1970s.

It wasn't just singers and musicians that Mick McCarthy booked to perform at The Embankment. He had some top plays staged there as well. 'McCarthy did unbelievable things up there – putting on plays, including works by John B Keane, which were hugely popular with audiences. He even got Micheál MacLiammóir to perform at The Embankment,' says Paddy.

Micheál MacLiammóir, the internationally acclaimed actor and playwright, lived and worked in Dublin in the 1960s and '70s. He co-founded the Gate theatre with his partner Hilton Edwards. He wrote many plays and appeared in numerous one-man shows, which he also penned. One of his most successful one-man productions was *The Importance of Being Oscar*, based on the writings of the famous Irish poet and playwright of the late 1800s, Oscar Wilde.

'I went with McCarthy to where MacLiammóir lived, and we interviewed him in his back garden,' says Paddy. 'McCarthy convinced him to go out to Tallaght, saying that it would be like what Oscar did by touring in the wild west of the USA. Oscar Wilde went out to the American west and did shows there. McCarthy was saying if Micheál came out to the countryside in Tallaght, it would be like when Oscar went out to the cowboys in America.'

He convinced MacLiammóir to do so, and Paddy got the honour of being the support act for him at The Embankment. 'In my mind's eye now, I can still picture MacLiammóir saying, "I'll do it, but this young man has to open for me." I thanked him, and said, "I will be delighted to do so, sir."

He squeezed my hand very tightly and replied, "If you ever call me 'sir' again, you'll never father a child." It was the best way of saying "I'll give you a kick in the bollix" that I ever heard,' laughs Paddy.

He remembers others, including comedians Noel V Ginnity and the late Brendan Grace, and Scottish comedian and singer Billy Connolly, performing in The Embankment. 'Noel V used to come to the bar on the Saturday night to sing songs as well. Noel, or Noddy as we called him, played the spoons also. Noddy and I started, and Gracer came to The Embankment with a music group called The Gingermen.

'Brendan was a singer, who started to do more talking and telling jokes on stage than singing. He was a great singer – and I don't just mean that he was able to sing; he was a real good singer,' says Paddy sincerely.

While many have claimed to have got 'the start' at The Embankment, both he and Brendan Grace definitely started there, around the same time. 'Brendan was only a young fella. Grace was ten years younger than me when he took off, as a comedian more so than as a singer, and life for him changed too.

'Brendan became a great friend of mine and we did a lot of touring together from the early days right up to recent years. Gracer and I did concert tours together in Australia eight times,' he says. 'Australia is a country where concerts start early and finish early, unlike the sessions in The Embankment that didn't always end at the official closing times!

'There was no such thing as a night – there was only dawn, only days. The birds were hoarse from singing when we were going home from The Embankment,' laughs Paddy.

Scottish comedian and singer Billy Connolly visited The Embankment during the early days of his career, but he couldn't get a gig there! 'I remember Billy Connolly being up in the bar there one night and he was trying to get a gig off Mick McCarthy, but it wasn't happening. Mick even brought him into where I was singing, and he told Billy that he couldn't sing like that.

'When Billy became famous, on the "Michael Parkinson Show", Connolly never let McCarthy forget about the time that he wouldn't give him a gig. Years later, he would come out to The Embankment to slag McCarthy off, because he wouldn't give him a gig. By that time, he was a million-dollar man,' laughs Paddy.

Billy Connolly did come back and perform in The Embankment in the 1970s, and the crowds loved him. 'Billy is a nice fellow, and we always got on well together. He has toured the world, and has told me many stories about his experiences abroad.

'One of the funniest tales he told me was regarding when he was touring as support act to Elton John in America. Elton's fans just didn't want to hear Billy. They were there to see the star of the show, and not the support act. "I was about as welcome as a fart in a spacesuit," laughed Billy Connolly when telling me that story,' roars Paddy.

Paddy remembers other famous people at The Embankment, and one who found it difficult to even get into the venue. That was Art Garfunkel of Simon & Garfunkel fame.

It was a case of mistaken identity that stopped him getting in, as Paddy relates:

'Well, Tommy Makem was there, after inviting Art Garfunkel out, and we were all waiting in the bar. There was panic when McCarthy said, "Some fecker was trying to get in free at the door earlier; he said he was Garfunkel or some such name." Wild panic set in!

'It was Art Garfunkel, and it was snowing the same night and he had let the taxi go. When he couldn't get in, he had started walking back towards Dublin. That was on the Blessington Road at perhaps three o'clock in the morning. Sure, there wouldn't be anything moving on the Blessington Road until eight o'clock, and even then, it would only be a sand lorry,' says Paddy with a laugh.

Somebody from The Embankment jumped into a car and went after him along the Blessington Road. Paddy says Art was 'drenched' wet when they brought him back to the venue. But once he got inside the warm venue and with a warm welcome from everyone, including McCarthy, the near-disaster came to a happy conclusion.

Christy Brown, of *My Left Foot* fame, also frequented The Embankment during Paddy's tenure there as an entertainer. 'Yes, Christy used to come a lot. Mrs Brown lived in Crumlin, and she used to bring him up often. He wound up buying a house near here that Tos Taaffe built, and Christy came to live in Rathcoole then. But Mrs Brown used to come to The Embankment and bring Christy there long before that. I also remember there was another girl who used to drive him to The Embankment in a Morris Minor car. Christy Brown and Mick McCarthy were good mates. He did a couple of lovely paintings that he gave to Mick that were in the ballad room. I would have loved to have gotten one, but I never did,' says Paddy.

He also remembers the playwright Brendan Behan walking around Rathcoole village occasionally. But Paddy knew Brendan's mother far better from her frequent trips to The Embankment.

'She became a great friend of mine; Kathleen Behan was a character. She used to come out to my gigs in The Embankment. Johnny McEvoy and Mick Crotty and some others were also often playing on those shows.

'Mrs Behan was in a retirement home at that time, but a son of hers from her first marriage, Rory Furlong, used to bring her to The Embankment. She always had a fun time, and she would stay singing until three in the morning.'

While he got to know Kathleen Behan, Paddy admits that Luke Kelly and Ronnie Drew knew Brendan Behan and Patrick Kavanagh much better than he did. He also says that it seems that Behan and Kavanagh had a dislike for each other.

'Well, Behan hated Kavanagh, because Kavanagh was very successful, at a time when Behan hadn't anything. Kavanagh was lecturing in the Sorbonne during that time, and he got Behan to paint his apartment on Raglan Road. He painted it black – windows, doors, furniture, even the television, everything black.

'Luke enjoyed chatting with all those guys such as Paddy Kavanagh and Brendan Behan. He would be with them in the pub as they were arguing with each other,' says Paddy.

Paddy says that Patrick Kavanagh had a dislike for the Irish National Anthem, simply because it had links to Brendan Behan's family. 'Paddy Kavanagh used to love going to the races in the Phoenix Park. He was coming out of it one day, running, and they were playing the National Anthem. The Artane Boys used to play in the gazebo at the side of the parade ring at the races.

'They were playing the National Anthem when the races were over, and Paddy Kavanagh was coming out when somebody stopped him to stand for the National Anthem. "What I would be doing standing for a whore of a march written by that bloody Brendan Behan's uncle?" is said to have been his reply,' laughs Paddy.

Ronnie Drew sometimes frequented the same pubs in Dublin as Patrick Kavanagh – but they weren't always admitted to two pubs in Baggot Street! The Crooked Bawbee was one, and Searsons was the other, but many of those pubs have changed names several times since then. Anyway, it was near both pubs and on the bridge that Patrick Kavanagh and Ronnie bumped into each other one day. Their conversation went something like this:

"'How are you Ronnie? How's it going?"

"All is good Paddy. How are you?"

"'We'll go for a drink; let's go to Searsons,' says Paddy.

"'I can't go into Searsons," says Ronnie. "I'm barred. Let's go over to the Crooked Bawbee."

"'I can't go into the Crooked Bawbee, I'm barred from there," replied Paddy.

'They were the only two pubs open in the area at that time of day, but the boys couldn't go into either bar together! "Ah, good luck, Ronnie, I'll see you again," was Paddy Kavanagh's concluding remark,' according to Paddy Reilly.

As the 1960s rolled on towards the '70s, Paddy Reilly's friendship with his contemporaries such as The Dubliners, Shay Healy, Danny Doyle and Pecker Dunne grew. Paddy looks back with a laugh and says, 'Many of us were related through drink.'

However, some music writers say their alleged fondness for 'the grog' may have been exaggerated. Most of them were entertaining in pubs anyway, and drink usually featured in photographs and films from that time. Singers in other musical genres were fond of drink also, and drugs were becoming a growing problem with entertainers, especially across the water in the UK.

Drug abuse hadn't manifested itself to any great extent during the ballad boom years of the mid- to late 1960s in Ireland. But Paddy agrees that drink was ever-present – and not only in photos of gigs or in the words of songs. 'Yes, there was serious drinking on the music scene, and that is not an exaggeration,' he says.

Perhaps the international success of 'Seven Drunken Nights' by The Dubliners, or 'Whiskey You're The Devil' and 'The Jug of Punch' by The Clancys, or Paddy's 'The Craic Was Ninety In the Isle of Man' glamorised the porter and the whiskey in the jar! But, while drugs were off the radar, the craic that those balladeers partook in during the 1960s included drinks they enjoyed in the pubs and clubs where they played.

As the 1960s drifted into the '70s, the days of having the craic and the porter black, while playing around his native Dublin, would soon end for Paddy. He got an offer he couldn't refuse – work as an entertainer in America.

'I had no intention of being a full-time singer in Dublin, let alone America. But Mick McCarthy in The Embankment horsed me into it, and renamed me Paddy Reilly. He horsed me into leaving my job in the paper mills also. A few years later, when I got that offer to go to America, I took it. There I met my good wife and another chapter of my life started,' says Paddy.

Chapter 3

Life and Love in America and Ireland

To paraphrase the words of one of Paddy's most popular songs, the craic was ninety in Dublin in the late 1960s. The ballad scene had been booming since the middle of that decade, and it spawned many superstars. These included The Dubliners, The Wolfe Tones, Christy Moore, Jim McCann, Danny Doyle, Johnny McEvoy and, of course, Paddy Reilly.

Paddy says he became a singer 'by accident', but it's obvious that getting a foothold in the burgeoning ballad scene in Dublin was the foundation for his future working life. Those early days were fun times too, with a plethora of parties every week around the city.

The offer of work as an entertainer in America in late 1968 was one

Paddy, Noel Ginnity (seated), Jim and Phyl McCann, Danny Doyle, Johnny McEvoy and Andy Irvine.

that Paddy couldn't refuse, even if his parents would have preferred if he did refuse it!

'My mother thought I was going off in some sort of coffin ship and they would never see me again. Like the rest of us, she didn't know that the times were changing fast. Luke came to Dublin Airport with us, and up to then my mother had never drank alcohol in her life. But Kelly gave her brandy to try to appease her after my departure,' he says.

'My father kept asking, when would I get a "proper job"? He thought that we were all mad in the music business, and maybe there was more than a grain of truth in what he was thinking!'

For a while, Paddy had combined working in the paper mills with gigging in The Embankment and at Dublin cabaret venue The Old Shieling in Raheny. Dolly McMahon, wife of the famous presenter of traditional music programmes on RTÉ Ciarán Mac Mathúna, organised the entertainment at The Old Shieling.

'Jim McCann and I were the sort of top-of-the-bill artists. But she would also have an Irish session musician playing, ten-minute opening spots, before we came on stage. You will laugh when you hear the names of some of those support musicians. Two of them later became internationally famous as members of The Chieftains – Paddy Moloney and Matt Molloy.'

But when America came calling with an offer to Paddy Reilly, he quickly left all this behind. 'I never regretted doing what I did. Once I made up my mind to do something, I could always be pretty decisive,' he says.

Even so, he still activated a safety net, asking one of the bosses at Saggart Paper Mills if he could return to his former job if his music career didn't work out.

'When I told one of the foremen there that I was thinking of leaving to go full-time in the music business, I also asked, if it didn't work out, could I have my job back? I was doing okay working in the mills, and was a number-one man in my department in the paper-making business.

'The foreman's response was that he couldn't guarantee my job back if the music didn't work out. But he said he would give me "some job in the mills" if the music didn't take off. Then, with a loud laugh, the foreman added, "Now, go on and do what I didn't do. That means get to hell out of here!" It seems that I took his advice,' says Paddy with a smile.

'I had got into a singing career by accident – it was never a calculated thing by me. Only for Mick McCarthy in The Embankment, I wouldn't have got into it at all and then, quite suddenly, I was going off to America as a singer.'

His father's advice fell on the deaf ears of the young Paddy Reilly. 'He thought we were all mad to be in the music game, and he would say, "When will you give up that singing and get yourself a proper job?" He continued with that observation all his life.'

But Paddy's mother was more circumspect on him going into a more volatile working life as an entertainer. 'My mother was full of the more "fair-haired boy" stuff – I couldn't do any wrong in her eyes,' he laughs.

'Ah, to get to America and get away from shift work – I thought I had died and gone to Heaven. And a few of the other lads who were singing here in Dublin came out afterwards. Boston was good; I enjoyed it. I got gigs then for the summer. Later in my career, I was also working summers in Cape Cod, which was lovely.'

Paddy had been spotted at both The Embankment and The Old Shieling by promoter Mike Broadbine, who owned several pubs. These included The Harp and Bard in Danvers, a town in Essex County, Massachusetts, about fifteen miles from Boston.

'It would have been about '68 or '69 or thereabouts when I got the chance to go there. Mike had already brought out The Blarney Folk to

Paddy singing in The Harp and Bard in Danvers, outside Boston.

play in his pubs. They had recommended me to him, and that is how Mike contacted me and asked if I would go out there to play.

'I enjoyed the freedom of America, and America was very good to me. Apart from playing in The Harp and Bard, I also went down to New York to play in a few Irish bars in that city. I also worked around Washington DC for a few years during my first and subsequent trips to the States, and I loved it. I met good people down there too. I had good times working for a man named Danny Coleman, who owned The Dubliner, a pub in the Phoenix Park Hotel on Capitol Hill. This was frequented by many top US politicians, including Senator Ted Kennedy and Tip O'Neill.'

Life in New York, Boston and Washington DC was in the modern fast lane, but Paddy discovered that it was a far more normal environment than an area in Canada where he went to visit some relations.

'I went to visit cousins of mine in Canada, as my father's brother was the only one that emigrated from our family in that generation. He was in the British Army in India and Africa before he settled in Canada. They lived in a place outside Toronto, and it was like dangerous jungle territory. There was a sign on the door into the local pub stating, "Check your guns and knives before ordering your drink." It was hunting country.

'I don't know whether my Canadian cousins were hunters, or if they were being hunted, but it was a tough place.'

One of his cousins had a wild horse that nobody could ride, but Paddy, with his background working in Taaffe's stables as a youth, was willing to break the horse in!

'I saddled him up anyway and got the gun plus the saddle bag, and off I went shooting gophers. I thought I was John Wayne,' says Paddy.

While playing in Mike Broadbine's pub, The Harp and Bard, Paddy met his future wife, Diane Blythe. She was a beautiful-looking and talented lady from Massachusetts. Diane didn't have any Irish ancestors – her people were mostly of German extraction. But it seems that when she saw him on stage and heard Paddy sing, it was love at first sight.

'She worked in admin, as secretary to the President of MIT College in Boston. She came to the gig that night and we became friends quickly, and it developed from there. We got along from day one – or night one,' he laughs.

'She also became such a help to me behind the scenes. Yet it was by chance that she came to that gig in The Harp and Bard.'

In an interview with Kay Doyle in *Ireland's Own* magazine in 2019, Paddy says how quickly he was smitten by her beauty. 'It wasn't hard to spot her,' he says with a smile. 'She was a very stunning woman … Once we got to know each other, we teamed up, moved in together, got married, had a family and it all moved along naturally.'

However, Paddy says that ending up with a roving singer like him must have taken Diane out of her comfort zone. 'I took the poor woman away from the lap of luxury in Boston to live in a noisy apartment over The Old Shieling in 207th Street, the Bronx, New York. That must have been such a tough change for her. But she soldiered so well with me.

'My wife came from good stock. I won't say well-to-do people, but they certainly weren't wanting, and she winds up with this itinerant musician! There we were, living beside the elevated subway in the Bronx. The trains rattled through it every three minutes, and the pub downstairs operated all through the night.

'The song playing in the jukebox in the pub down below is one that I will never forget – they must have played it every five minutes. It was the Lynn

Anderson hit of the time, "I Never Promised You a Rose Garden". It must have been on some sort of automatic rewind on the jukebox in the pub, just below the room where we were trying to sleep. The pub opened at ten in the night and never closed till ten in the morning. I felt like going downstairs many times and breaking the jukebox open and stealing the disc that the "Rose Garden" song was on,' laughs Paddy.

'Diane was pregnant with our daughter Ashling at that time, and our living conditions were atrocious. I put her through Hell, moving there from the lap of luxury in her family home! But we eventually moved out of New York and went back to Boston, where Diane had a luxury apartment. When we moved into that apartment, I commuted to my gigs from there. At least it took her back into some remnant of civilisation.'

Their baby daughter Ashling was born in the USA, and so also was their son Ciarán, two years later. 'They are both pretty close in age, and we were lucky to have moved back to Boston, as there was no way we could have reared them in 207th Street in the Bronx. It was also a changed environment there at that time. What had previously been a predominantly Irish area was suddenly being populated by mostly Puerto Rican emigrants as the Irish, including us, moved out.'

Paddy wasn't the only Irish star to serve an apprenticeship in The Old Shieling pub in 207th Street – tenor and actor Colm CT Wilkinson also played there with him in the early 1970s. 'Colm and I worked there at that time, a while before he got his big international break with *Les Misérables*. After that he did *The Phantom of the Opera*, and became an international superstar on stage. But before all that happened for Colm, he paid for his sins playing in the pub on 207th Street,' laughs Paddy.

When Paddy and Diane came to Ireland to get married and set up

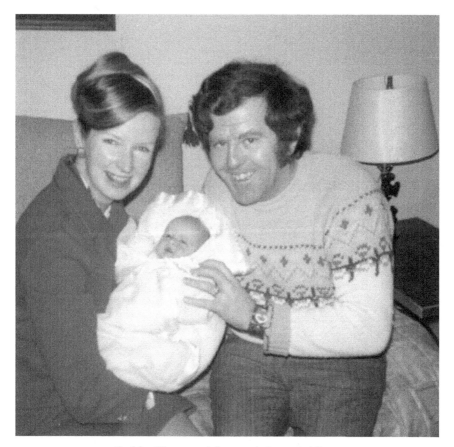

Paddy, Diane and the newly born Ashling.

home in his native area, it was her first time in Ireland. 'We came back here to get married, as my parents were very Catholic. Our wedding ceremony was in Saggart Church,' says Paddy.

Their wedding was a big one, with a lot of celebrities in attendance, as Paddy explains:

'The celebrations went on for a week. All the friends from the music business were there – Luke and Ronnie and John and all of the Dubliners were among the guests. It was Diane's first time in Ireland, and she certainly arrived for a hooley,' he laughs.

Paddy and Diane on their wedding day, 1970.

A large crowd of people turned up to watch the wedding celebration and to see the celebrities that were in attendance. In his 2019 interview in *Ireland's Own* magazine, Paddy says that most of the onlookers weren't there just to see the wedding couple. 'A lot of people turned up at our wedding to see The Dubliners, not me! And sure, we all got up and played for the dance too. The wedding was in The Embankment, where it had all started.'

Paddy says his children are lucky to have both Irish and American citizenship. But he wanted them to be born in America for another reason also. He recalls with sadness how his parents and family were so traumatised when his sister Linda died at twenty-six. Sadly, Linda died while in hospital for childbirth. If it had been in the present time, or if it had been in the UK or the US, she might have been saved. Paddy was only a teenager at the time.

When Paddy and Diane and the children moved home to Ireland, they initially had a small cottage in Rathcoole. 'We lived in the little cottage in Rathcoole for a while, until we had raised enough money to build a bigger home, which the family still own. Our son Ciarán and his wife and children live there now. I moved out to a smaller home when he got married, as I was away on the road a lot of the time anyway. It's great that the next generations of the Reilly family still live there,' says Paddy.

Rathcoole was a small village when Paddy returned from the States to set up home there. He wasn't going back to a job in the paper mills, and so to support his young wife and two children, he threw himself at full throttle into the Irish cabaret scene.

'The ballrooms were closing and the latest music scene that was springing up was in cabaret lounges and hotels. There were venues in almost every town in every county in Ireland, north and south.'

His name was getting well known all over Ireland in the early 1970s, after the release of his first solo album, 1971's *The Life of Paddy Reilly*. This was followed by a second solo album, *Paddy Reilly at Home*, the following year.

In early 1974, Paddy had his first number-one single with his version of the Phil Coulter song 'The Town I Loved So Well'. The song enjoyed three spells in the Irish charts over a five-year period. Paddy Reilly was suddenly in demand – not just around his native Dublin, but all over Ireland.

Paddy recorded for many record labels as a solo artist and later with The Dubliners. But he was probably most prolific recording with Dolphin and Harmac. Other labels included Tribune, Topic, Capitol Records (Canada) and Ritz (UK). However, Paddy views some record company executives and some managers with more than a molecule of cynicism.

'I wasn't too aware of the business end of the recording scene. I assume that when some of those songs were released in England, perhaps Mick Clerkin of Ritz leased them from Dolphin. But I don't know, as that was the business side of the scene, which I wasn't aware of at all. I was just a pawn; I wasn't the king. Most managers and record company executives are only aware of money. We were the meal tickets for them,' he laughs.

He admits though that his management had input regarding making recordings and getting him onto several TV shows. He jokingly says that before he went away, he was only on TV 'two or three times'. When asked what programmes he was on, Paddy with his quick wit responds, 'Oh, I made a few appearances on "Garda Patrol" on RTÉ.' This was the forerunner of the 'Crime Call'-style shows of today!

Paddy is lavish in his praise for Gay Byrne, who he says 'took Ireland out of the dark ages' with his 'Late Late Show'.

At a Harmac Records album launch (left to right): Brendan Harvey of Harmac Records, singer Seán Ó Sé, Paddy and former Tánaiste Brian Lenihan.

I'm not just saying that because "Gaybo" put me on the "Late Late Show" after I came back from America. I'm saying it because I mean it. Gay Byrne was a gentleman, and the best talk show host ever. He was better than all those people I saw presenting TV shows in America – Johnny Carson and all the others, getting millions of dollars for what they did, and they couldn't shine Gay Byrne's shoes.'

He also has great memories of being on "The McCann Man" TV series with his contemporary Jim McCann.

'The LP *The Life of Paddy Reilly* was the first album I ever made. It was a mix of songs that I enjoyed singing and that were popular at my live shows when I moved back to Ireland.'

While it contains a few Irish rebel songs, Paddy never had an emphasis on rebel songs. Of course, being the son of a man who fought in the Irish War of Independence and the Irish Civil War, it was inevitable that some rebel songs would appear on Paddy's albums. On his debut album, the rebel tracks were 'James Connolly' and 'The Irish Soldier Boy'.

Another song takes a humorous look at both sides in Northern Ireland: 'The Orange and the Green'. This song pokes fun at the religious differences of the Irish. But Paddy couldn't care less about religious differences anyway.

He was one of the few singers from the south who continued to play in Northern Ireland right through the Troubles, but he had to be careful with the songs that he sang across the border. 'I got into trouble a few times up there for not singing Bobby Sands songs. But at the time, I didn't even know that Bobby Sands had written songs, as I had been away in America for a few years. I got into a little bit of hot water over that, but that was only with some die-hard republicans. I played in "no-go areas" during the height of the Troubles, such as the Ardoyne and similar places.'

During the Troubles in Northern Ireland, one person who praised Paddy Reilly for continuing to play in the north was Sinn Féin leader Gerry Adams.

Paddy had to be extra careful where he parked when playing in Belfast during the bombings. 'I never drove all the way into the "no-go areas". I would have another car hired to pick me up at The Crown pub, right opposite the Europa hotel in Belfast.'

This old-style Belfast pub is still his favourite bar in the world. 'I love the old gas lights and the snugs that are still there. They were introduced in many pubs to keep the women out of the main bar in the olden days – strange times.'

Of course, Paddy's hit recording of 'The Town I Loved So Well' took him to Derry for more than just a photo-shoot for the album cover. He also befriended the late John Hume and his wife Pat. Indeed, Paddy and Diane Reilly and John and Pat Hume used to holiday together in Donegal during those years.

'"The Town I Loved So Well" was so controversial, because of what happened in 1969, during the Apprentice Boys' march in Derry. That was the beginning of the Troubles, and John Hume stood on the walls of Derry and gave his famous oration. What he said that day he continued to say for the next forty years. He never changed his tune. At that time, Gandhi would have been my man of the century, but as the years went by, John Hume became my man of the century.

'He was one of the greatest pacifists of all time. His wife Pat was a great support for him – just as the old cliché states, "Behind every great man is a great woman." She was a lovely person. My wife and I used to go on holidays in Donegal many years ago with John and Pat, as well as with Phil Coulter and his wife. We all became very good friends. John Hume was a saint and a genius to continue to stand by what he said from that first day at the walls of Derry for the next forty years of his life,' says Paddy.

Luke Kelly also sang an iconic version of 'The Town I Loved So Well'. Over the years, Luke always remained a singer that was loved so well by Paddy, his wife and Paddy's mother. They even got him to eat occasionally!

'My mother and my wife were among the few people that could get Luke Kelly to eat a full meal. There was also a lady in Manchester called Kath Corless who could get him to eat as well. But from the first time that I got to know him, and then after I came back from America, I can never remember him eating much. Even when he would get a meal in a restaurant, he would just chase it around the plate. He wasn't inclined to eat a lot due to the drink, and it was hard living.'

Paddy notes that Luke gave up the drink in the later years of his young life. This is also mentioned in an excellent 2020 cover story titled 'Remembering Luke' in *Ireland's Own* magazine.

Paddy also knew Ciarán Bourke from the early days going to see The Dubliners playing in Howth, and in the years afterwards as well. 'I knew Ciarán well, but unfortunately he got a massive stroke while still young and he couldn't talk or do anything. It was very sad. He was such a talented man but, like Luke, he was hard on himself too.'

'I have memories of Luke getting up in the morning at ten o'clock and going straight to the pub. He would walk the short distance from where he lived to the Leeson Lounge. However, sometimes he liked to go golfing with me,' says Paddy.

As well as liking going golfing with Paddy, Luke also took a liking to an expensive banjo that Paddy had bought while in America. 'I don't think he ever bought a banjo,' says Paddy. 'The one he was using he had got off a fella from Glasgow, and he never gave it back to him. Then he was after giving Liam Clancy a couple of songs such as "The Wild Rover", and some others, and Liam bought him a banjo.

'Luke had that banjo from his early days in The Embankment in the 1960s, and for many years afterwards. But he decided to fall in love with my very pricey banjo. I bought the long-armed Pete Seeger banjo for a thousand dollars almost sixty years ago – a thousand dollars back then was like fifty thousand dollars now.

'It was a wonder my wife didn't kill me for buying it, but once Luke got a hold of it, I couldn't get the banjo back off him. They were playing at The

Embankment, and he said he had lost his banjo, or he came out without it. Whatever the excuse was, he came looking for my banjo, and somehow or other I didn't get it back.

'Luke travelled the world with my feckin' banjo, and it was only when he was in *Jesus Christ Superstar* that I managed to get it back, by going to his house when he was out,' laughs Paddy. Luke starred as King Herod in the rock opera *Jesus Christ Superstar* in Dublin's Gaiety theatre in 1973.

'I went to his house, and there was another man who lived there, Brian Peters from Belfast, and I got the banjo out of the house from him when Luke was on stage. He never got that banjo again,' says Paddy with a laugh.

He remembers, with great fondness, another time when Diane and he helped Luke prepare for another starring role. 'The song "Scorn Not His Simplicity", written by Phil Coulter about his child, was immortalised by Luke. Kelly and I were out playing golf earlier on the day when he was due to perform that song on TV.

'We got soaked to the skin and we were so muddy when we came back that Diane had to throw the two of us into the shower to try and clean us up,' laughs Paddy.

'We had to go to The Embankment for the filming of "The McCann Man" TV show that night. Luke did a very moving and heartfelt rendition of the song. There was a copper awning over the fireplace they were sitting around as he was singing, and the camera shot was of the reflection from the copper awning – it was very clever and artistic. It showed Luke in a very emotional stance, with his head bowed while singing the song.

'The truth of the matter was that while he was showering back at our house earlier, Diane and I wrote out the words in large letters for him. He hadn't had a chance to learn the lyrics to the song yet, as Phil Coulter had just written it. But we had written it out for him in large lettering on a sheet that he left discreetly on his knee. As the camera only showed his head bowed, everyone watching his TV performance spoke of the emotion with which he sang that song.'

Diane was also a talented artist, and no doubt the lush green fields and rolling hills near their home in Rathcoole were an inspiration for her paintings. 'Diane was a very good painter, both in watercolours and in oils,' says Paddy.

Music and songs by Paddy and paintings by Diane went hand in glove in their years together in Rathcoole. However, he says that while she liked all types of music, Diane wasn't that familiar with Irish music, apart from The Dubliners, until she met and married him. But sure, in doing so, it turned out that she married a Dubliner anyway!

'Oh my God, sure my songs were shoved down the poor woman's neck! She wasn't particularly musical, but while she would have enjoyed music, she wouldn't have known much about Irish music until we met,' laughs Paddy.

Paddy says he was so fortunate to have had such a great wife. Sadly, Diane passed away all too young, in 1998 and only in her mid-fifties, during the years when Paddy was a member of The Dubliners.

'But she has left me with two of the greatest kids that you would find anywhere in the world. My daughter Ashling lives in Boston and my son Ciarán lives here. We miss her every day, and we are very close, and we all love one another,' says Paddy.

They had many happy trips to America during his second period of playing there, when he had become better-known as an entertainer. That was after becoming internationally famous for his definitive version of

'The Fields of Athenry' and later 'The Flight of Earls', also an anthem for the young Irish in the US and elsewhere in the 1980s, another decade of chronic emigration.

Chapter 4

Highs and Lows in London and Elsewhere

Paddy was at the pinnacle of his career when he played in London's iconic Royal Albert Hall. It was one of the most memorable shows of his career. But he had to inform another promoter in London that playing in an Irish ballroom there, during the demise of the dancehalls, was not what the dancers wanted!

The Irish boys, immortalised in The Dubliners' hit 'McAlpine's Fusiliers', might have great craic in the Irish ballrooms of London, but those dancehalls were fading fast by then, and their decline was terminal.

Attempts at life support by some ballroom proprietors included booking a solo singing star such as Paddy to perform in them, but this wasn't always the solution either.

By the time Paddy was playing the Irish scene in London and other English cities, he had a number one record at home with 'The Town I Loved So Well' and a slew of best- selling albums under his belt.

He was also making guest appearances with The Dubliners from time to time, whenever one of the regular line-up had to drop out from some show due to illness or other reasons. 'I was always the first sub on The Dubliner's team, sometimes when Ronnie or Luke might be sick or maybe in jail,' he says jokingly.

Another sub on The Dubliners team from time to time was the late great Jim McCann. McCann was a contemporary of Paddy's on the solo ballad/folk scene and a close friend as well. In 1972, when Paddy had one of his most successful early albums, Jim McCann wrote the glowing sleeve notes for the record, released on the Dolphin label.

Jim, who had his own career song 'Grace' over a decade later, summed up Paddy Reilly very well in those sleeve notes:

'It is generally considered the ultimate in professionalism when a performer can catch the attention and affection of an audience within minutes of taking the stage. I don't think Paddy Reilly knows how or why but he does it every time. The affection is freely given because it is so obviously mutual. When Paddy chats to an audience, those listening feel that they could just as easily be chatting to him over a pint. Which in fact is true.

'Who could fail to be attentive when he switches moods from a table-thumping rebel-rouser like "Come Out You Black and Tans" to a moving and sincere rendering such as his version of "The Ballad of Joe Hill".'

McCann added that as he penned those lines, Paddy Reilly was in America.

'Over there, apart from his very evocative name, he epitomizes everything that is best in Irish music and song to those home-sick Gaels on the far side of the Atlantic. We, of course, are spoiled. We can see and hear the man from Rathcoole whenever we want to!

'We can't see Paddy Reilly on this album, but we can hear him. And that's not so bad, is it?'

Many decades later, another of Paddy's great friends, and a touring partner, the late Brendan Grace, would express similar sentiments in his 2009 book *Amuzing Grace*:

'Paddy is by far one of the best singers that I know. He and I became a double act for years, touring Australia and Canada. Paddy was particularly big in Australia, and he was always a sure-fire bet to bring in a large crowd as his records were constantly being played out there.'

Paddy was always delighted to go to London and sing his songs for the Irish there. But the showband scene over there was declining at that time as the cabaret scene was coming in.

'The Irish emigrants in the 1970s and '80s still liked to hear me singing songs such as "Deportees", even if they wanted jives, slow sets, waltzes and similar stuff from the band that might be on stage after me.

'That mix ensured that they could ask the girls on the other side of the hall out to dance, as they would have done back in the ballrooms in Ireland.'

Paddy's ballad singing co-existed happily with the bands in most of the Irish ballrooms in Britain and he enjoyed playing there. But there was the occasional time when it didn't work out. One incident stands out very vividly in Paddy's mind to this day. It was in Camden Town, an area famous for dancing during that era.

'The ballroom was The Buffalo, and I was on a fee of £100 for the night. But after doing one or two songs, I said to the promoter that playing to that crowd was pointless as they wanted to dance. I asked would he give me £50 and let me cut my act short and go home.

'They were all after probably hearing some other solo singer, or maybe a group, singing those songs in the Irish pubs before heading to the ballroom to dance the rest of the night away.

'All they wanted to do there was to make a beeline for the girls on the other side of the floor and hope to find the love of their life. The promoter said he would give me £40 if I was going to cut my show short. I took it and called a cab, and went back to where I was staying in London,' says Paddy.

But that was a rare exception. On most occasions, the combination of ballads and showband hits worked well. And after 'The Fields of Athenry' became a hit, Paddy headlined his own shows at some of the biggest ballrooms and clubs in England. He played sold-out shows in the prestigious venue Blazer's of Windsor. Paddy also has happy memories of playing in the Irish ballrooms in the UK, ones such as The National in Kilburn.

'Any time I am over at race meetings in the London area since then, I usually meet up with the Carey brothers who operated that ballroom,' he says.

Paddy Reilly continued to play in London, and had a huge fan base there, 'mostly among the Irish', for the following three decades. One memorable gig as in one of the city's most prestigious venues, the Royal Albert Hall.

'That was one of the greatest experiences of my life,' says Paddy. 'I had never been in the Royal Albert Hall till the night I walked out on the stage there. I just couldn't believe the size of the place and its layout. It's the most magnificent auditorium in the world, and I've played in a lot of them since.

'The Royal Albert Hall was special for me. I believe that one of the music critics who was reviewing my performance there in an English newspaper quoted what I remarked when I went out on stage. Before I sang a note, I said, "Jesus, you could stack some hay in here," and the crowd burst out in laughter. I was so terrified going out there, but I think my mention of putting hay into the hall calmed both myself and the audience, and I had a great time and loved the gig.

'The Royal Albert Hall will always remain special in my mind. I have never been in it since. But I've been trying to get tickets for the Proms there. I've never been to the Proms, but my son Ciaran is hoping to organise tickets for me to go sometime soon.'

The BBC Proms have been staged in the Royal Albert Hall every summer for the past forty years. They usually feature approximately thirty orchestras and ensembles, totalling about 2,000 musicians. Most years there are over fifty performances at the Royal Albert Hall.

Paddy has almost all good memories of playing the many Irish ballrooms, pubs and clubs around London, which he did for nigh on thirty years. He also loved being out on the town in London, and later in Manchester and Birmingham, with some of the Irish soccer stars of that era.

But a zany British pop act, named The Wombles of Wimbledon, rehearsing above a room where Paddy was trying to sleep didn't enhance his early views of the UK capital!

'The Wombles were rehearsing either for a Christmas pantomime or else for an appearance on "Top of the Pops". It was unfortunate for me that they rehearsed in a room in London over where I was trying to sleep while recovering from a bad flu.

'I was staying in The Irish Club, as I often did, but from 9.30 every morning till five in the evening all during that week, the sound that was coming through the ceiling of my room didn't help my flu! It went something like "two three four, bump, bump, bump, overground, underground". A fellow playing the same tune all week, and I was so sick I couldn't get out of bed. It went on incessantly and I nearly lost my feckin' mind,' laughs Paddy.

Was it a bit like the jukebox downstairs in the pub in the Bronx, playing Lynn Anderson's 'Rose Garden' almost continuously? 'It was on a par with it,' Paddy roars in reply. 'But at least I was on my own in London – I wasn't putting my poor wife through Hell, like when she had to listen to "Rose Garden" almost every five minutes in New York.'

For those of us of a certain age, The Wombles were a manufactured pop group that emerged from a BBC children's programme. Created by British singer and composer Mike Batt, three of their spin-off novelty songs were UK top-twenty pop hits in 1974. These were 'The Wombling Song', 'Remember You're A Womble' and 'Banana Rock'. Paddy Reilly was never likely to record versions of either Lynn Anderson's 'Rose Garden' of any of The Wombles' songs. He remembers both acts for all the wrong reasons!

Paddy has had some great times around London with several Irish soccer stars, and some even wilder times partying around Birmingham and Manchester with other Irish soccer stars and a snooker ace.

'I spent some good times, mostly outside of London with stars such as Niall Quinn, Frank Stapleton, Liam Brady and Pat Jennings, who were

Arsenal players. But they were outside London – Highbury is not really London,' he laughs.

Irish soccer star Ray Treacy was a good friend of Luke Kelly, and also a friend of Terry Corless, who owned The Circus bar in Manchester. Paddy and Luke sometimes stayed here and fraternised with many of the Irish soccer stars in England.

'Luke used to stay with them. As I said earlier, Terry Corless's wife was one of the few people that could get Kelly to eat. My wife and my mother were others that could do so. Apart from them, nobody else could get food into him. I don't know how he lived as long as he did, because he lived on drink, and not on food,' recalls Paddy in a sad tone.

Both Luke and himself loved the craic in The Circus bar, Manchester, a favourite spot for Irish soccer stars in that area. 'Oh my God, all the lads went in there, all the football stars of that time, including Bestie (George Best). But sure, there wouldn't have been many places that he hadn't drank in,' says Paddy with a laugh.

'George was a lovely fellow and a real gentleman, and everybody got on with him. Even Paddy Crerand, who played with Man United at that time, and didn't always get along with Protestants, got on great with George Best – he was sometimes referred to as Best's minder. Others have described him as the Roy Keane of his day, who didn't hold anything back, either on or off the field.

Paddy Crerand was a native of Glasgow, but his parents were from Ulster, and he played with Glasgow Celtic before moving on to Manchester United. The religious bigotry he faced growing up a Catholic in the tough Gorbals area of Glasgow may have given him the incentive to try to help resolve issues during the Troubles in Northern Ireland. According to his autobiography, *Never Turn the Other Cheek*, he was friends with John Hume, as Paddy Reilly was, and he talked to Martin McGuinness of Sinn Féin to try to resolve a rent strike in Northern Ireland in 1975.

One incident that stands out in Paddy Reilly's mind is when he sang an Orange song for George Best at a party in a Manchester Hotel.

'We were in the Britannia Hotel in Manchester, and everybody was singing rebel songs. Bestie was there and he had a pain in his bollix from listening to them all. He said, "Will somebody sing 'The Sash'?" and I got up on the counter and sang it. Then I marched up and down after I sang the song, and he loved me for that. Bestie's people were Orange Protestants to the hilt.'

Paddy says Manchester was a great town to be in around that time, but a tough town too if you were in wild company, such as that of snooker ace Alex Higgins. 'Alex Higgins would be around with Ray Treacy sometimes. I signed him into the Playboy Club in Manchester, and he got us all thrown out; he nearly got us all arrested,' laughs Paddy.

Paddy also loved playing gigs in Birmingham, where he was often a guest of another Irish soccer star, Johnny Giles, and his wife Kay. 'I would often stay with them, and they were very nice people. Gilesie lived in Edgbaston, and I used to stay in their house, with the bedroom overlooking the very posh Edgbaston Cricket Club.

'Giles went to West Brom, and he brought all the Irish players – Paddy Mulligan, Mick Martin and Treacy – back to Birmingham when he got the job as player manager of West Brom.'

When touring in London, Paddy would usually stay at The Irish Club, which was in Eaton Square, Belgravia, until 2003. During that era, some Irish actors used to stay there as well, including the late Donal McCann, best known for his role in John Huston's film *The Dead*.

'A lot of Irish entertainers and actors stayed there around that time. The accommodation was cheap; there was a bar there, which was open most of the time, which was the main reason! I became friends with a lot of lads in the game who were fellow drunks, like Donal McCann and those boys. McCann and I became great friends. We were related through drink,' laughs Paddy.

'All the entertainers who stayed in that Irish Club then were big drinkers, and I mean everybody,' says Paddy. 'McCann arrived in the club once after a massive pay day for acting in a BBC production, with £5,000 sterling in his pockets, and he started to drink.' This would not normally startle Paddy, as they often drank together. But when he heard McCann say that evening that he was going greyhound racing in White City, Paddy knew that would have disastrous consequences.

'Donal had got that money from the popular BBC TV serialised adaptation of Anthony Trollope's "The Pallisers". Going to the dogs with the £5,000 in sterling in his pocket, and he drunk at the bar in The Irish Club already, required me to take drastic action. I said to myself, "Ah good Jaysus, what can I do quickly?" Well anyway, I did a lot of bullshitting around him, and eventually I got the five grand off him. I didn't pick it out of his pocket and while I can't remember how I did it, I got the money off him anyway. I left him about 200 pounds. The rest of the money I brought with me to my gig for safe keeping for giving back to him the next day.

'I went off doing the gig up in Kilburn or maybe it was Camden Town, and it was really, really, rough up there that night. There were so many boys knocking the bollix out of each other, and I was on stage singing there in the middle of all that.

'The next day, I was in the bar of The Irish Club, having a cup of coffee, getting ready to go to the airport. McCann comes down from his bedroom at twelve o'clock, looking wrecked. He said, "Are you going home?" and I replied, "Yes, are you going home?" He said he was going home on a later flight. Then I asked him how he did at the dogs. He responded in a despondent tone, saying, "I lost all of the fucking money, or else it was stolen from me at the dogs." He thought he had lost all the money in White City.

'So I said to him, "Wait here a minute, I have to go back to my room for something." I came back down and handed him his five grand, and he couldn't believe it. Otherwise it would have been gone. He would have lost it on the dogs, because McCann was a gambler. He was accustomed to betting, as his father was a bookie. But betting in that drunken state would have been disastrous. At least he could go home with his money in his pocket.'

Sadly, despite his ability as a brilliant actor, Donal McCann battled with drink issues and depression for much of his life. He died from pancreatic cancer in 1999, at the age of fifty-six.

Paddy says that the image portrayed in the media at that time of balladeers as hard drinking men was not an exaggeration. Internationally, The Dubliners seemed to lead that image, with photographs usually showing them with pints in their hands or at least in close proximity to drink!

'The image wasn't an exaggeration. There was a lot of drinking among balladeers in those days. Sure, when working in Ireland, I would arrive back from gigs in Mayo or somewhere like that at 3.30 in the morning, and I'd go straight to The Embankment. I would get in and we would stay there until the daylight hours.

'The Dubliners were hard drinkers too, especially in the early years. But not by the time I joined them in the 1990s. At that stage, I was the only one of them that was drinking.'

Paddy's parents were non-drinkers. He says that even when he had achieved success as a recording and performing artist in the 1970s, his dad would still not go to see him play in a pub.

'He wouldn't go into a pub, as he was very anti-drink. I heard that he used to drink at one time, but I can never remember him drinking. He did go to some of my earlier gigs in Liberty Hall, but that's all. My mother liked to come to the gigs, and she was nice singer as well,' he adds.

Both Jack and Nellie saw him achieve his first number one with 'The Town I Love So Well', and he had toured in America and in England before they passed away. 'My mother died in 1980, and she was only seventy-five, but my dad lived on to eighty-six, and he died in 1986. They were very close all their life. But they had a hard life and people didn't live to such a big age back then. After my mother passed away, my father used to say, "Wasn't she an awful woman to go and die and leave me on my own?" That was one of his regular lines then,' says Paddy.

It is unlikely that Paddy's parents would have approved of the hard drinking that went on in the Irish pubs and clubs of London in the '70s and '80s when he played there.

While some of the actors, singers and musicians that Paddy hung around with when touring in England had drink issues, most of the soccer players were far more circumspect in their consumption of alcohol.

'The Irish soccer players that I was friendly with in England were all good lads. They had gone over to English clubs when they were only thirteen or fourteen years old. It was Luke Kelly that introduced me to Ray Treacy and both Luke and I often stayed with him. He was with West Brom, but the boys that I knew from home who were with Arsenal were great friends of mine also. Ray Treacy was a pal of mine for life,' says Paddy.

His friendship with Ray Treacy lasted until Ray died after a short illness in 2015 at the young age of sixty-eight. Apart from his talent as a soccer player, he also set up Ray Treacy Travel, and was the official agent for the FAI. He helped thousands of fans follow Ireland all over the world. Ray organised many of Paddy's trips around the world for gigs.

'Ray was a great pal of mine. When I was doing all the cabaret work around Manchester, I would often stay with Ray. He was very good to me in those times and often drove me to and from gigs in the UK.

'Then, when he came home to Ireland after his playing days were over, we always remained friends. Ray also loved to get up and sing, and he had a banjo and he fancied himself as a player of that too.

'I used to wind him up at times, saying, "I knew Ray Treacy when he used to sing for Swindon Town," and he hated that,' laughs Paddy.

'As Ray went to play football in England when he was probably only twelve or thirteen, I didn't know him in Dublin when he was growing up. But our friendship started when he was a soccer star in the UK.'

Both Paddy and Ray were pranksters, and he recalls how the two of them had an involvement in taking a limo used by Keith Richards of The Rolling Stones during one of their trips abroad. 'It was more Treacy than me that engaged in that prank. We were going to New York, and we got grounded at Shannon Airport when something happened to the plane.

'Keith Richard was on the flight with us, and Marianne Faithful was with him. We had to stay overnight in a hotel, before going on from Shannon the next morning. A limo was parked outside the hotel to take Keith and Marianne back out to the airport. When I told Treacy that it was there for Keith Richards, he told the driver that I was Keith Richards. He believed him, and Treacy and I rode out to the airport in their limo; I don't know how they got out afterwards,' laughs Paddy.

'Treacy, as a travel agent, was flying free, as travel agents did in those days if there was a spare seat. But the change of flights caused some problems with that. The next day, there wasn't a spare seat for Ray on the rescheduled Air Lingus flight to New York. He was offered a free seat to New York via Newfoundland on an Aeroflot flight. I switched my flight to travel with him, but I didn't know at the time that we would be flying via Newfoundland. It was the scenic route to New York,' laughs Paddy.

He was going to the US to play, and also for business reasons – to do with a bar in New York, appropriately named Paddy Reilly's. It is still there, on 2nd Avenue in Manhattan, and has live music seven nights a week, four of those nights featuring Irish acts.

Paddy purchased the bar with a colleague from the music business and a promoter of Irish acts in the States, Steve Duggan. Duggan was also a former Cavan football star of the 1960s. Paddy remained involved with the business for several years, but sold out to his business partner almost three decades ago. When asked how, or why, he got involved in the pub business, Paddy's quick-as-a-flash reply is, 'Sure, everyone wants to own a pub.'

Steve Duggan used to also promote many of Paddy's tours in the States, and Steve and Paddy are still good friends. But did Paddy ever play in the New York pub that still has his name over the door? Was he ever a hands-on innkeeper there, perhaps even collecting glasses or working behind the bar?

'Yeah, I played there many times, but regarding other work there, well, all I can say is that I worked very hard on the customers' side of the bar,' replies Paddy good humouredly. 'It's a great live music venue for local bands and for touring musicians coming to New York city.'

However, having been a part-owner of a bar for several years, he is not upbeat about being in that business. 'It's a business for fools if you don't know what you are doing. Everybody thinks that he or she can run a bar, but it doesn't work that way. Being a bartender, or being a bar owner, are professions in themselves. The fact that you play a guitar and sing Irish songs doesn't give you the qualifications to do it – believe me,' he adds emphatically.

But at least in a bar anywhere, be it America or Ireland, you must pay for the drink you order. Sometimes, as a musician, at the end of the night, you can have difficulty collecting your fee. Over the years, Paddy has had a few arguments with innkeepers and promoters in order to get paid for the hours he performed at their venues. None sticks in his mind more than one west-of-Ireland bar owner who wouldn't pay him until he stole his prize racehorse – for a while!

'When the gig was over, there was no sign of the owner, who was supposed to pay me. So I stayed over that night and went around to visit him in his house the next day.

'He had a racehorse stable, and when I couldn't get him at his house, I went to the stable. There was a youth there looking after the horses, and he said, "He's not here." So I said I was interested in buying a racehorse and I asked, what was the best racehorse that he had?'

The youth didn't suspect that Paddy wasn't as interested in racehorses as he seemed.

'I said, put a halter on him and walk him out till I have a look at him. Then I said, I'll take him for a quick walk till I see him moving a bit more, but I'll put him back in shortly.

'So I headed out the Dublin Road from Sligo, with the horse in the halter behind me. I hadn't walked too far when this Land Rover pulled up alongside me and the driver shouted, "Where the hell are you going with my horse?" I replied with an expletive regarding my fee. We had a short argument, but I got paid there on the side of the road, and he got his horse back.'

There was no horsing about with Paddy when somebody tried to dupe him for work that he had done, and rightly so.

Chapter 5

North America, Ted Kennedy and Brushes With the Law

Like so many other Irish people, Paddy became a success in America. He has great memories of his sojourns there – plus some humorous, embarrassing and scary moments too.

He got to play in one of the most prestigious venues in the States – Carnegie Hall, New York, a highlight in any artist's career. Paddy became close personal friends with Senator Ted Kennedy and Speaker Tip O'Neill in Washington DC. Senator Kennedy and the Reilly family became particularly close during those years.

During his visits to the Library of Congress on Capitol Hill, Paddy's life-long love of reading really blossomed. He could be found there regularly whenever he had downtime away from playing around the Washington DC area.

Paddy is a voracious reader, so much so that Brendan Grace, his travelling partner on many tours, wrote that it was a misnomer to just say that Paddy Reilly has a guitar and will travel! The Gracer, as Paddy affectionately called him, wrote in his autobiography that a book was the only baggage Paddy wished to have, even on trips to Australia:

'Paddy was extremely anti-luggage. Hand luggage for him was a book. I always reckon that if there had been such a thing as an inflatable guitar, Paddy would have been the person who invented it'.

Paddy laughs out loud about that. 'Grace was always slagging me about that. I'm a reader of all sorts of books, but I suppose I started with reading books about Irish history. I am a reader of more factual books than of fiction but I would often read a good thriller too. Like, who wouldn't read a thriller by Robert Ludlum?'

The late Robert Ludlum was a multi-million-selling American writer, possibly best-known for creating the character Jason Bourne from the original The Bourne Trilogy series. His works, mostly spy fiction, thrillers and mystery, are published in many languages and some have been adapted for film and TV.

The Library of Congress might seem like a strange setting for a touring Irish singer in Washington DC, and Paddy says that going to a library was an almost alien experience for him at first.

'I was always a reader, but wouldn't be a regular for visiting libraries until I was working for a few years in Washington DC. That's where I discovered the Library of Congress. To be honest, I had never attended school very much as a youngster, and I didn't really know how to get into using a library. I used to stop the students and ask them questions regarding where I should go to read specific books in the Library of Congress.

'It is the most unbelievable place, and apart from the books there is also so much microfilm there. I just love the place, and eventually I got into using it regularly – there is such a mine of information there about everything in the whole world.'

Was he mostly educated in the University of Life? He hesitates for a moment, but doesn't disagree. 'Well, there's that in it too. I enjoyed my learning on the streets and stages of the world.

'A lot of the stuff that I've read in the Library of Congress would be on American themes and on the history of the States. I've read so many American books that the list is very long by now. Some were great books about people who have done so well in the US, including those of Irish descent like the Kennedys. Others were sad books such as *Bury My Heart at Wounded Knee*, which I read a few times. It is one of the most heart-breaking books one could ever read.'

Back home in Ireland, Paddy has been keeping up his schedule of reading, very often into the early hours of the morning. 'Oh! I still wait until two or three am at times, because if a book is a good one and a page turner, I will keep turning the pages till I have read it all.

'I read books about the atrocities that went on in Irish history, especially in the years leading up to the Easter 1916 Rising and during the War of Independence and our Civil War. Another subject I've read about is what went on in Dublin between 1910 and 1914–16 regarding workers seeking their rights. What the poor people of Dublin went through then was terrible. They were starved into submission. I read books about Jim Larkin and James Connolly – they were two marvellous men.

'The Easter Rising became such a total cock-up, such a tragic misunderstanding of the whole issue; the cause was defeated even before it occurred. We know from our history that whatever moves were due to happen during that Easter weekend were cancelled at the last moments. Those who went ahead with the rebellion were left in a bad place because of the divisions of beliefs which still range through to this day among many Irish.'

From earlier years, Paddy has read about Michael Davitt and the struggle of the Land League in the late 1800s. Paddy says he was delighted to find, during one of his tours in America, evidence of Davitt's long-lasting impact on Americans during his campaign there to support the rights of Irish tenant farmers.

'There is even a club in Detroit called The Land League Club, even though it is not a city that has many people of Irish ancestry. Much of the population there are of Afro-American heritage. But Davitt reached out to all in America and got support for the struggles of the Irish during his US trips. He was an amazing man,' says Paddy. Davitt's work is immortalised in a museum about his life in Straide, Co. Mayo, where he was born and laid to rest after his death in Dublin in 1906.

Paddy Reilly's reading has continued across a wide spectrum of subjects, from the Irish Land League to the American Civil War and more. 'There is so much to read about in America, and they disagree on politics as much as we do in this country. My love of reading was certainly nurtured there during my visits to the Library of Congress, and I continue to read books on American or American-Irish topics.

'Recently my son Ciarán bought me a great book about JFK. It gave me a great insight into the amazing amount of work that Kennedy did, and it wasn't just concentrating on stories about the women in his life. I was so fed up reading books about Jack Kennedy's female conquests that I wasn't even going to read that JFK book that my son bought for me,' he laughs. 'But that book gave a great insight into the plight of the Irish and the Jewish people in some parts of Boston around the time that his grandfather first arrived there.

'JFK's father, Joe Kennedy, fought hard to move those people up the ladder of society. He was a very strong man, especially during the reign of Roosevelt. Kennedy called all the shots during Roosevelt's time in the White House. But Joe Kennedy never wanted to be President of America. He was so happy to be the Irish-American man representing the States in the country's embassy in London.'

When asked if he reads books about his heroes, the Dublin football team, the quick-witted Paddy retorts, 'I should have been writing books about them.'

'The first time ever I went to the west coast of America was with the Dublin football team. I had worked before on the east coast of the USA, but we went to San Francisco then, and we had a great time. I'll say no more about it, as I don't want to be giving away secrets about any of the players. All I will say is that they were all well-behaved,' he says with a wry grin.

America became a great place for Paddy to play in the late 1970s and early '80s. With major hits under his belt back home, his fame was also spreading among Irish-Americans.

'I was flying to and from gigs in America during the late '70s and the 1980s more often than an Aer Lingus pilot,' laughs Paddy. 'I suppose you could say that I was one of the pathfinders for Irish solo folk and ballad singers going out there. I would have helped colleagues in the business such as Danny Doyle and Jim McCann to get gigs in places that I had played in.

'When I was a little more affluent, we were able to stay in Manhattan. Eamon Doran's bar was a great drinking and meeting spot for many Irish and Irish-American people in New York. I loved it and we missed it so much. Eamon was a gas man. There was a big picture of him inside the door of the pub and a big smiley face on him,' says Paddy.

He also loved playing in Cape Cod, and Diane and the kids would travel out when he was doing summer seasons there. 'The summer season in Cape

Paddy, Diane, Ashling and Ciaran at the Shannon Door restaurant in New Hampshire, 1976.

Cod was ten weeks, from Labour Day to Memorial Day. The kids were off school for weeks, and everybody moved out from Boston to Cape Cod. I'd play five nights a week there for ten weeks. There was nothing easy about working in America, because they judge you by the amount of time you are on stage rather than what you do.

'I would do three or four forty-five-minute shows each night. Sometimes I would also do other gigs on my nights off. But there was a great holiday atmosphere about the Cape,' he says. 'I met great people there. I became great friends with Lou Rebesa, who built the Falmouth Country Club literally with his own hands. We became great friends and he used to come over here on holidays and stay with us. He also became friends with my sister Jean and all; it was great. He was one of the greatest characters I ever knew.'

While he loved Cape Cod, it seems that Washington DC was Paddy's favourite place of all in North America. 'One of my favourite gigs was The Dubliner on Capitol Hill in Washington DC, where I played for five years. When I was moving on, I got Jim McCann the gig there and he liked it too,' he says.

Unlike the words in the Garth Brooks country hit from the '90s, 'Friends In Low Places', Paddy had friends in high places in the States. One of these was Senator Ted Kennedy of the famous Irish-American Kennedy dynasty. Another was Tip O'Neill, Speaker of the United States House of Representatives for a decade from 1977, when Paddy's popularity was also on the rise in America.

Like the Kennedys, Tip O'Neill was a proud Irish-American, as his grandmother came from near Buncrana in Donegal. Apart from their Irish roots, the Kennedys and the O'Neills were inextricably linked through Democratic Party politics. Tip won the seat in the US House of Representatives vacated by John F Kennedy in 1953. When he retired in 1987, after being re-elected sixteen times, he was succeeded by Joseph Kennedy II, a son of former Senator and former Attorney General Robert Kennedy.

During a conversation with Paddy Reilly on one occasion, Tip jokingly remarked that he went to Harvard University, just as Ted Kennedy did. 'Tip was a gas man; he said that when he went to Harvard, it was for a different reason than Kennedy. He said he went there to cut the grass,' laughs Paddy.

Senator Kennedy attended Harvard University and later the University of Virginia, from where he graduated with a law degree. He was an attorney before winning a Senate seat in 1962, which he held until his death in 2009. He and Tip O'Neill were both hugely influential politicians in the USA around the same time. Paddy has great memories of both of them socialising in venues where he was playing in Washington DC, and of personal friendships with both.

'Tip was a very influential man. He used to be in The Dubliner often when I would be playing there. There was a pub next door to the Dubliner called The Irish Times, and Tip used to frequent that pub also,' he says.

'I loved Washington DC. I had a great time there, even though I spent most of my time, when not on stage, in the Library of Congress. It was a great time in my life. I often met Ted Kennedy and Tip O'Neill, and Ted and I became great friends. He was American-born, but I always regarded him as a good Paddy. He liked to have a drink, and we had many together. Like Tip O'Neill, Senator Kennedy was proud of his Irish roots, and they both did so much for the peace process in Northern Ireland.'

Senator Kennedy became friends with all the Reilly family, and there is a framed photograph that holds pride of place in Paddy's home of them all together.

Family photo: Paddy, Ciaran, Diane and Ashling with Ted Kennedy on
Capitol Hill, 1984.]

'On one occasion, Diane, Ciarán and Ashling were in the USA during
Ashling's thirteenth birthday, and Teddy Kennedy took us to lunch to celebrate her birthday. That was when we had all our family pictured with him.

'We all had a lovely time with him. He brought Diane, myself and the
children to his office that day as well. Ted was a nice fellow. Much of his
effort for the peace process in Northern Ireland was coached by John
Hume, I might add.

'Ted Kennedy and I had many good times together, although I was in his
house one night when he wasn't there and I drank half a bottle of bottle of
vintage wine, which some friend had given him as a birthday present and
apparently cost $1,500.

'I was there with his German chef and another person who worked for Teddy. I had no idea of the cost of the bottle of wine that we cracked open. Because I had had a few other drinks earlier that day, I probably didn't think about how valuable a bottle of vintage wine might be. Sure, at that late time in the evening, I didn't care either about what it cost,' says Paddy, laughing out loud. 'Ted never forgave me for doing that. However, we didn't fall out over it.

'Teddy Kennedy was such a nice man, and so, so Irish – as were all of the Kennedys. I was in the homes of several of them. Everything about them was Irish, and they were so proud of their roots.'

Among other famous people that Paddy befriended in the US was Ruby Bridges, the first African-American child to go to an all-white elementary school in New Orleans, Louisiana, in the southern United States. She made history as a six-year-old in doing so back in 1960.

A framed photo of Ruby with Paddy is prominently displayed beside that of Teddy Kennedy on a cabinet in Paddy's home in Rathcoole. He is proud to talk about his meeting with her and that she attended some of his gigs in the States.

'She was a great lady. I met her in New Orleans. She came to some of my gigs and I got to know her well. When President Obama was in the White House, he had a famous painting of her by the American artist Norman Rockwell, which he borrowed from her, hanging in the Oval Office. Obama said he would not have been there only for people such as her. I have a copy of that painting hanging there in my front hall,' Paddy proudly proclaims.

The painting is of white people taunting the little girl and throwing objects in her direction on the day she became the first black child to attend the all-white school.

'Another friend was the Chief Justice in New Orleans at that time. She was Ginger Berrigan, an Irish-American lady, and it was she that introduced me to Ruby first. We all went out to dinner together. They were lovely people.'

Was Ruby a fan of the Irish ballads that Paddy sings? 'Well, she liked the civil rights aspects of many of them anyway,' he replies.

Of all the venues that Paddy played in during his tours of America and Canada, Carnegie Hall in New York was the most iconic. Carnegie Hall is one of the world's most famous concert halls, its stages having been graced by many of history's greatest artists and public figures.

Opened in 1891, it is known for its excellent acoustics and extravagant architecture. On 5 May 1891, hundreds of New Yorkers jammed the concert hall to see the great composer Tchaikovsky play there, according to the website manhattan.com. The construction of the venue began in 1890, financed by Andrew Carnegie, one of the richest men of the time. It is built in the Italian Renaissance style, its elegant foyer a vision of marble and intricately carved columns.

Paddy Reilly may not have known all about its illustrious history when he was booked to play there. But as a voracious reader, he had already researched some of the famous names who had played there in decades past. He knew that he was one of only a select few of his peers from the Irish folk and ballad scene to have the honour of playing there.

'To play in Carnegie Hall was incredible, unbelievable – those are the only words to describe it. It was an amazing experience, one of the highlights of my career. The first non-classical act ever to play in Carnegie Hall was The Benny Goodman Swing Band, back in 1938. Benny Goodman was there with his band of mixed races playing jazz tunes like "Sing, Sing,

Sing", in what was once a puritanical concert hall. That was a big thing for jazz music back in 1938. I was there on stage on my own, years later, singing Irish ballads and folk songs, just me and my guitar, and that was some experience too. The Wolfe Tones and The New York Police Pipe Band also played there that night.

'When I got a standing ovation after singing in Carnegie Hall, I just said to myself, now I know how Benny Goodman must have felt when he played there. Oh my God, it was a truly amazing experience.'

The mid-1980s saw another wave of young emigrants going from Ireland to America in search of work. Once again, a song sung by Paddy Reilly, 'Flight Of the Earls', became an anthem for them.

'It connected with so many young people going to England as well as America in search of work in those times. It was a very successful song, for both Liam Reilly, who wrote it, and for me. Once again, like 'The Fields of Athenry', I think the 'Flight Of the Earls' song also picked me rather than me picking it,' laughs Paddy.

'Liam, who was no relation, wrote it and I think he asked me to record it, and when I did so it became a hit. It was a very poignant song for Irish emigrants, especially those in New York. The city was full of young, illegal emigrants from many countries at the time. Only a small number of the young Irish ones were legal.'

Liam Reilly was the frontman with the group Bagatelle for years, and the composer of many hits. Apart from 'Flight Of the Earls', songs with emigration themes include 'The Streets of New York', a massive hit for The Wolfe Tones, and 'Boston Rose' for country singer Mike Denver. He also wrote and sang hits with his own band, such as 'Summer in Dublin', 'Second Violin' and 'Trump Card'. Liam passed away at sixty-five in January 2021.

Radio and TV presenter Terry Wogan, jazz saxophone maestro
Paddy Cole and Paddy.

When playing for emigrant Irish-Americans in North America, Paddy
didn't just tour in the United States. He also toured in Canada on many
occasions. Several of his albums were released there, right back to the
first one that he ever sang on from his Embankment days. The album
The Gatecrashers, featuring Paddy, Danny Doyle, Shay Healy and Pecker
Dunne, was released on Capitol Records (Canada) as far back as 1967.
Paddy exclaims that 'it escaped'!

'I must have played in almost every town and village in Canada as a solo
artist. None of the places I played in Canada would be as cosmopolitan as New
York. As Canada is such a big country, there are vast areas that are not populated. I liked playing on the west coast of Canada, but not so much in Toronto
on the eastern side, which I always thought seemed to be very colonial.

'There were a lot of divisions in Toronto, because most Irish emigrants who couldn't get into the US went to Canada. Of course, northern Protestants had no problem getting into Canada, because they were British citizens.

'There were different stages that I went through playing in Canada. I gigged in some really rough places earlier on, but then, as I got better-known, the standard of gigs went up. Overall I enjoyed playing in America and Canada,' says Paddy.

The Irish built the railroads on the east coast of Canada, but it was the Chinese that did so on the west coast. 'There was a big influx of Asian people on that side of Canada. Not that they would be coming to my gigs, but I would be going to theirs, as I love their food,' laughs Paddy.

One of his favourite places to play in Canada was Newfoundland. He was amazed at how so many people there spoke with Irish accents. 'I played often in Newfoundland and did well there. It amazed me to hear people there who, even though they had never been to Ireland, were talking with Irish accents. Some of them spoke with what I thought was a mixture of Dublin and Wexford accents. Others had accents that sounded like they were from Waterford or Tipperary, and it seems that's where their ancestors came from,' says Paddy.

Perhaps that is why those Newfoundland natives would pack venues there to see Irish folk acts such as Paddy, The Fureys or Foster & Allen. Paddy recalls a brush he had with the law when he was playing there, along with The Fureys. Paddy was playing that night in St John's, the capital of Newfoundland. He did the first half of the concert, with The Fureys doing the second half.

Paddy hired a taxi to take him back to his hotel after he had finished, but the taxi driver arrived early to watch his show and he got drunk.

Paddy had to drive him home in his taxi, and a police car took Paddy to his hotel afterwards!

'The taxi driver hadn't drank in years and, after a few jars, he wasn't able to drive. I drove him home in his taxi and, as he lived a few miles outside the town, I started walking back to my hotel.'

That was when Paddy suddenly saw blue lights flashing.

'It was a police car, and they pulled in beside me and they said, "Don't you know it's an offence to be walking in a public place with alcohol on you?" I replied that it was lucky they didn't meet me five minutes earlier, as I was driving a cab!

'They thought I was being a smartass at first, until they discovered that I was in town doing the concert in the Arts Centre earlier. The police then drove me back to the hotel I was staying in, and they drank the contents of the mini-bar in my room,' he laughs.

It wasn't the only strange brush with the law that Paddy had during his tours in North America.

'I got this old banger of a car for $50 from a Kilkenny man who had a little garage in Boston. It was okay for me just for driving to and from gigs while I was there. Then when I was out playing golf with a friend of mine, he offered to lend me his new Buick LeSabre car for a night. It was a beautiful vehicle, but as we were late getting back from the golf, I had to take him to his shift work first that night and then I had the car to go to my gig.'

Paddy was driving back to his hotel in style from his gig at one o'clock in the morning when he was pulled over by the police.

'The first things they asked for were my licence and registration. I didn't know if there was a registration in the glove box of the car, but I knew that my licence was in my old car, back at my apartment. While I was trying to explain that to the policeman, his colleague jumps into the passenger seat and starts tearing the dashboard out of the car.

'The other fellow took me out and had me spread-legged across the bonnet of the car with a gun to my head. I had no identification, and that is an offence in the US. I was trying to explain to him who I was when a few lads who had been at my gig earlier came along in a car. They pulled up when they saw my plight. Apparently there was a serial number inside the dashboard of the car and it had been tampered with. So, the car I was driving had been stolen.'

The lads who had been at Paddy's show earlier offered to vouch for his identity to the police officers.

'One of the lads ran back to their car and brought over an album they had bought off me, which I had autographed. They were shoving the album in front of the cop's face, but he still had a gun to my head. He wasn't happy about what was going on, as they were obstructing his vision.

'They kept saying, "That's Paddy there on the album, officer," but the policeman wasn't impressed. He retorted, "Listen, guys, I'm a cop, not a goddamn disc jockey." At that stage, I just fell down on my knees laughing,' says Paddy.

Eventually Paddy was allowed to go back to his apartment, but the police confiscated the car and the man who had given the loan of it to Paddy never saw it again. He was unaware that the car had been stolen and fitted with false number plates – he had been given a false registration when he bought it.

Chapter 6

'The Fields of Athenry' Found Me

Many versions of 'The Fields of Athenry' have been recorded – almost 100, including some in different languages. But the definitive recording is by Paddy Reilly. Others have also had hits with it, but the undisputed fact is that Paddy took 'The Fields' to the world. He even took the song outside the world, and into outer space!

Sport has also been a big part of Paddy's life and coincidently his biggest hit, though not a sporting song at all, has become inextricably intertwined with various sports, such as Gaelic football, soccer and rugby.

Paddy says that 'The Fields of Athenry' is the song that changed his life, but he is somewhat blasé about his own input into this life-changing hit. 'I didn't find "The Fields" – "The Fields" found me,' is his nonchalant and self-effacing response to the question about this massive hit.

Paddy refuses, point-blank, to give his views on earlier versions, by the likes of Danny Doyle or The Barleycorn. 'That's a very unfair question, and I refuse to be drawn into any discussion about other versions,' says Paddy with a wry smile.

He says he had no idea that he had a hit on his hands after recording it, saying that his manager, the late Jim Hand, insisted that the song, recorded for an album, should be released as a single.

'If you knew what would be a hit,' says Paddy, 'you would never record a miss. It was a great song, written by Pete St John, but I was just recording it as a track for an album. We went into the studio with fourteen or sixteen songs, mostly ones that I selected, and "The Fields" was among them.

'After we recorded it, Jim said that it would be a hit, and he was right. He picked it out as a winner, and I replied that it had been recorded before, as I was aware of other versions of it being out there already. But he said it didn't matter and that we should go with it again. I never thought that my version would be the most successful.

'Pete St John and I got along very well – he is a laid-back guy like myself, but he is such an amazing songwriter. I was delighted for Pete that it was such a success too. But for me, it just changed my life completely. I went from playing in pubs for £50 or £60 a night to playing in theatres all over the world.'

One big change was the appearance fees his manager could now get for him following the success of 'The Fields of Athenry'. One of the major promoters of live music in the West of Ireland, Pat Jennings from the TF Royal Hotel and Theatre in Castlebar, Co. Mayo, has brought some of the biggest acts from all genres of music to play in his Mayo venue. He also

A hugely successful musical partnership: Pete St John and Paddy Reilly.

has some smaller acts, such as solo singers or up-and-coming acts, in the smaller venue at his entertainment and hotel complex.

Paddy had been playing in the smaller hall, before he hit the top of the charts with 'The Fields of Athenry'. Suddenly, his status shot up to that of a concert act. So also did his appearance fee.

'I used to drive down to Castlebar to play there for £50 or £60 a night. Sometimes I might spend more in the night than I would earn. I had to drive back home after all my gigs, no matter where I was playing in Ireland. I couldn't afford to stay over, as it would cost more than I would have earned for the gig.

'Pat Jennings rang my manager Jim Hand, regarding booking me for the big concert hall in Castlebar, and he asked what the fee would be. When Jim told him the cost, there was a lengthy pause on the other end of the line. I was in the office at the time, and Jim thought that the phone line might have broken down. So he shouted down into the mouthpiece, "Pat, are you still there?" and only then did Pat reply. His response was hilarious – he said, "I think those are the dearest f***ing fields in Ireland." We all laughed, and so did Pat. I played for Pat on many other occasions afterwards. He was a gentleman to work for, but I will never forget that remark.'

The late Jim Hand was Paddy's one and only manager. If he became a singer by chance, and got his biggest hit by chance, he also got his manager by chance.

'Jim was living in Raheny, and promoter Bill Fuller had the Old Shieling Hotel there, where I used to play. It was there I first met up with Jim and he convinced me that I needed a manager. That is how it happened. We always had a good friendship as well as a professional relationship. But I suppose in other terms, it could also be described as "honour among thieves" or something like that,' laughs Paddy.

His hit, selected by Jim, remained in the Irish charts for a staggering seventy-two weeks during 1983–84, but Paddy is fairly blasé about that amazing statistic too. 'Yeah, it was in the charts for something like that number of weeks. But it was simply a great song, written by Pete St John.'

He says the song just took off for him, 'even though it had been done by a few others before me'. Among the musicians on the recording session that produced 'The Fields of Athenry' for Paddy in 1983 was Bill Whelan. A little over a decade later, Bill was the composer of the seven-minute piece of music 'Riverdance', which was performed at the 1994 Eurovision Song Contest. Bill, along with Anúna, took that musical masterpiece to number nine in the UK charts also in 1994.

While Bill helped create the hit interpretation of 'The Fields' for Paddy, the earliest version of the song that got into the Irish charts was by the late Danny Doyle in 1979. The song got traction again in the charts in Ireland in 1982/83. Before Paddy's rendition became such a massive hit, the most successful version was one recorded by The Barleycorn. It reached number seven in the Irish charts and was in the top twenty for the group for seventeen weeks. That was shortly before Paddy's version spent its phenomenal seventy-two weeks in the charts.

Asked about the song's success, Paddy modestly says it was simply the luck of having the right song at the right time. 'As I've often said, you'd never record a failure if you knew what would be a hit. It was a "shot in the dark" type of thing. People took to my version.' With his hallmark grin, and a glint in his eye, Paddy adds in a jocose rather than in a bragging manner, 'Sure, maybe ours was the best one!'

After 'The Fields of Athenry' took off in Ireland, it did likewise in places such as the UK, America and Australia, as Paddy recalls. 'Yeah, it took off among the Irish, and people of Irish ancestry in all those countries. Of course, that made a big difference for me financially when touring abroad as well as at home.

'I even caused a traffic jam in Athenry when I played a gig there. The proprietor of the venue said to me, "Mr Reilly, you have caused traffic chaos in Athenry."'

His friendship with Dublin football trainer Kevin Heffernan produced a photo opportunity for Paddy as his song was climbing the charts. The Dublin footballers were training in Parnell Park in the lead-up to the 1983 final, in which they beat Galway. Dublin trainer Kevin Heffernan was very strict regarding anyone getting into those training sessions, but he made an exception for his long-time friend Paddy.

'I will always remember that year, because apart from the song becoming a hit, the Dublin football team won the All-Ireland. I went out to Parnell Park to Kevin Heffernan to get my picture taken with the Dublin team. While Kevin let me into Parnell Park for the photo, I'd safely say that I was the only one, apart from the team and officials, that ever got in through the gates there during those training sessions.'

Paddy doesn't hide his admiration for Dublin football teams, including displaying a specially engraved car number plate in the front window of his home in Rathcoole. The inscription proudly proclaims 'Dublin for Sam 2020'.

He says the six-in-a-row All-Ireland winners, under trainer Jim Gavin, were 'the best team that ever stood in Croke Park. I wouldn't know any of them young lads in the Dublin 2020 All-Ireland winning team; I wouldn't know Jim Gavin that well either. But I knew all the lads in the Dubs' "Heffo's Army" in the 1970s. Tooler and Keaveney and Hanahoe and all those lads were personal friends of mine.'

Paddy's support for Dublin football teams was ingrained in him from infancy – he was all of three years old when a neighbour trained the team to win an All-Ireland football final.

'Peter O'Reilly – who played for our club, St Mary's in Saggart – trained Dublin to win an All-Ireland in 1942, and there were five players from the club on that team. I was only three years old at the time, but Peter was a neighbour of ours and a hero in the area.'

Kevin Heffernan was one of Paddy's biggest sporting heroes when he was growing up, and a long-time friend of his in later years. 'Kevin Heffernan won fifteen Dublin Senior Football Championship medals and six Dublin Senior Hurling Championship medals. What Heffo did for Dublin winning the All-Ireland final was amazing.'

Paddy is also hopeful that Dublin Senior hurlers might emulate the success of their football contemporaries by winning an All-Ireland final sometime soon. 'But it is a lot harder in Leinster, as the province has so many top hurling counties – Kilkenny, Wexford and Offaly in particular. Dublin seems to be just one step below those counties in hurling. But they are there or thereabouts, and could come good one of these years.

'Sometimes a good footballer might also be a good hurler, but might opt for football. I remember two great Dublin footballers from the past – Des and Lar Foley – and what many might not know is that they were as good, if not better, at hurling. So also was Jimmy Keaveney; he was a brilliant hurler.

'There is a lovely story that I heard about how Jimmy came back playing football for Dublin. Kevin Heffernan used to give a lift to Mass to a kid who lived next door to him, who was only seven years old. One day Kevin Heffernan mentioned in the conversation in the car that Dublin were lacking a free taker. The little fellow spoke up and said that he went to all the St Vincent's matches with his dad, and that Jimmy Keaveney never misses a free. That's how Keaveney was brought back into county football, and the rest is history.'

It was in 1974 that Jimmy Keaveney made his comeback into the Dublin Senior team, having retired prematurely from inter-county football the previous year at only twenty-eight. As Paddy Reilly rightly recalled, it was Kevin Heffernan deciding to bring him back that saw Jimmy's impeccable place kicking help Dublin win All-Irelands in the 1970s.

Paddy says that while he follows Dublin hurlers, Gaelic football is his first love in sport. He says that the GAA is a wonderful organisation for every small village in the country that has a pitch to play on.

'In the old days, you might have to change in the ditch and get wet. They didn't have the facilities they have now. Most of the clubs now, whether in the cities or in the country, have nice dressing rooms and good social facilities too. It's the type of organisation that has saved eighty per cent of the youth in this country. Most notably in some inner city areas, where there were problems with drugs. Football and hurling, as well as other sports, saved their lives.'

But it wasn't the greatest disappointment of Paddy's life in 2021 when his beloved Dublin six-in-a-row team were beaten by Mayo in the All-Ireland semi-final in Croke Park.

'That wasn't a disappointment for me at all, because I was very glad that it was Mayo that did it. Dublin only just survived two replays with Mayo in the past, and only won each by one point. At that stage, there wasn't a team in Ireland, including Kerry, that could get within twenty points of Dublin.

'I was very glad that when they got beaten it wasn't by Tyrone or any other county. It was a very well deserved win for Mayo and I was delighted that it was them that did it,' he says.

Sports fans in many fields love to sing 'The Fields of Athenry'. It has become an anthem for many teams, even though it is not a sports song at all. Neither is it an old Irish folk song, or a song about emigration as some people mistakenly think. Both Paddy and the song's writer Pete St John are quick to assert the real meaning of the lyrics.

'Some people come up to me and say that it's a great rugby song; others say it's a great song about emigration; but it's neither,' says Paddy.

'Of course it's great that people listen to it or sing it for whatever reason they wish to. But it's simply a well-written tale about a young man being deported for attempting to steal corn to feed his starving wife and family during Ireland's Great Famine.'

The fictional young man in the song, named Michael, was trying to steal was 'Trevelyan's corn'. Charles Edward Trevelyan was a British civil servant, an Assistant Secretary at the British Treasury with responsibility for Ireland during the Famine. Under his watch, corn was being exported from Ireland while the Irish were starving to death. Trevelyan's name will always be infamous in Irish history for the export of native corn that could have saved many of the starving Irish. Later on, also during the Great Famine, he presided over the importation of an inadequate supply of Indian corn. But this was more suited for animals than humans. It was almost indigestible, and caused diarrhoea and scurvy among many who tried to cook and eat it.

Some of the desperate Irish who tried to steal 'Trevelyan's corn' – either the corn stored for export, or the inedible stuff from India – were caught and transported to penal colonies in Australia. While the Michael named in the song is a fictional character, Pete St John was told a story about a similar sad event that happened in Galway during Famine times. That was an inspiration for him during his research for the song, as he visited Athenry before his poignant story was put into verse.

In his website, Pete St John clearly outlines the origins of the song. He says he wrote it in the 1970s, and the Athenry in question is in Galway. 'If you do happen to get the chance to visit, you will notice the low-lying fields as you approach this beautiful town. The song is not a traditional song, even though it is written in that traditional style. It is a modern composition by myself, both lyrics and music.'

Professor Enda Delaney from the University of Edinburgh discusses the song on the RTÉ history website:

'Pete St John's inclusion in "The Fields of Athenry" of "Trevelyan's corn" – that is, food exported from Ireland during the crisis – made sure

Trevelyan's name would never be forgotten. Sung by Irish and Celtic football fans, it is the unofficial national anthem of both the Irish at home and across the Irish diaspora worldwide.'

Meanwhile, in *Irish Music* magazine, editor Sean Laffey succinctly states that 'Pete St John's "The Fields of Athenry" has become an anthem for the masses (after being brilliantly interpreted by Paddy Reilly).' He adds that it had become so 'in much the same way as the Corries' "Flower of Scotland" is now almost the unofficial national anthem of the Scots.

'Remember these were written when pop music was at its most pervasive, yet the folk quality of the songs has triumphed over the ephemeral fashions. The value of songs like "The Fields of Athenry" is truly priceless.'

'There is an excellent heritage centre in Athenry which is well worth a visit,' says Paddy. 'It will give the visitor a great insight into how this historic area inspired Pete St John to write the song.'

In fact, the Athenry Heritage Centre exudes history from the moment you lay eyes on it. It is located in the remaining part of the Protestant Church of Saint Mary, built in 1832, before the Irish Famine that inspired the song. The spire of that church casts its shadow on the surrounding ruins of the thirteenth-century St Mary's Catholic Church. The two churches, both venerating Saint Mary, are on the same site, and ironically epitomise the shared, if often fraught, religious history of Ireland. The spire of the Protestant church, and to a lesser extent the bell tower of the Catholic church, are visible in the distance from the low-lying fields of Athenry.

Alan Burgess, Director of the Athenry Heritage Centre, says he has met both Paddy and Pete, and the song about the fields has been a great help in encouraging visitors to come to Athenry. 'A lot of visitors from abroad, particularly soccer and rugby supporters, come here to the Heritage Centre because of the song. When they come here, they find a town steeped in history dating back to the thirteenth century.

'I was delighted to welcome both Pete St John and Paddy Reilly to Athenry in the past. We really appreciate how the international success of the song has helped attract visitors from all over the world to Athenry. They love to mingle with the locals and discover the town's historic past, and there is welcome here for all,' says Alan.

But not everybody was welcome to Athenry during its tumultuous past. In fact, some Irish chieftains had their heads chopped off when they tried to take the town from the Anglo-Normans in the fourteenth century! The town's famous walls date back to circa 1310, built by the Anglo-Norman settlers who established this outpost, bigger than Galway city at one time, in the middle of an area of Gaelic tribes.

Among the historic items preserved in the Heritage Centre are the Mace and Seal of Athenry. These were hand carved in solid brass after the Anglo-Normans defeated the Irish at the Battle of Athenry in 1316.

The intricate carving on the brass seal shows two heads on spikes over the historic entrance gate to Athenry. Alan Burgess explains how those heads became famous, for all the wrong reasons, long before 'The Fields of Athenry' was written.

'Both the seal and mace are originals, and are the finest examples of their kind from that era. There are no others like them on the island of Ireland. They were donated to Athenry by Captain Bilsheen, who lives in Richmond in the UK. They were handed down to him through the generations of his family, from the last chairperson of the Athenry Corporation, which disbanded in the mid-nineteenth century.

'As well as coming here to see the low-lying fields made famous in the song, many come to see these rare items. The two heads on the seal are those of the King of Connacht, Felim O'Connor, and local chieftain Tadhg O'Kelly. In the Battle of Athenry on 15 August 1316, they led the attack on the Anglo-Normans, and they lost to a man, losing an estimated 5,000 men. The Anglo-Normans chopped the heads off the Irish leaders and put them on spikes over the gated entrance to Athenry. That's why those heads are on the seal,' says Alan.

Of course, the song is about a totally different time in Irish history. But it was an equally horrific time for those who died, were deported or were forced to emigrate, during Ireland's Great Famine of the mid-1840s.

It became an anthem for fans of many different sports, firstly among Galway hurling and football supporters. Then it quickly became a hit with GAA fans from other counties around Ireland, and then GAA fans abroad. Others include fans of Munster Rugby, the Irish national rugby team, Glasgow Celtic and Liverpool FC in the UK. On the international rugby and soccer circuit, it's sung by fans wherever those Irish teams play around the world.

Paddy could never have envisaged, in his wildest dreams, that decades after he took 'The Fields of Athenry' to a world audience back in 1983, it would still be a world anthem for the Irish.

Back home in Ireland from 1983 onwards, the success of 'The Fields' for Paddy saw him play in some of Ireland's most prestigious theatres and concert halls. Playing sold-out shows for a week at the Olympia theatre in Dublin and a similar stint at the Gaiety theatre were personal highlights. Those concerts, as well as performing in the National Concert Hall and performing on RTÉ television, were all-time highs of his career after 'The Fields' made him famous.

'Aw, it was just such a thrill to be playing those gigs back in my home town,' says Paddy. 'It was nice to top the bill in the National Concert Hall in my own city; I was very proud of that.

'It was just a solo concert in the National Concert Hall; nobody else was on the bill but myself and we sold it out, which was great. Those shows all happened due to the success of "The Fields of Athenry". The National Concert Hall was a one-off, but the Olympia was for a week or two and we sold them out too. Yeah, I was good at box office stuff at that time.'

As he was scaling the heights of chart success and concert box-office success at home in Ireland, Paddy was also present later that year with some Irish soccer supporters when they spread the story of 'The Fields' in song across sunny Spain.

Paddy made that 1983 trip to Spain with Ray Treacy and thirty other friends and musicians for the Ireland vs Spain European Championship qualifier. But on arrival, the group, led by well-known Dublin publican Charlie Chalk, had to make a road trip 'in a half dozen cars' from Madrid to Seville to get to the match. They stopped off in Spanish villages along the way, having sessions and sing-songs in the squares, coffee shops and pubs with the locals.

'We were over for the matches, and we were in Madrid, but the match was in Seville and other places far away from where our flight landed. Charlie Chalk and a few others rented the cars and we went off the main highway and stopped at all these little villages.

'We visited pubs and coffee shops and sang the song as well as buying drinks for the villagers. Some of those parts of Spain, outside the main tourist areas, were very poor and those people had very little. The Spanish people that we met along the way learned the chorus so well, and sang along with us with such passion, that they almost turned "The Fields" into orange groves,' says Paddy with a laugh.

Paddy says that an emotional moment for him was when the Irish soccer fans sang 'The Fields of Athenry' for the Dutch team after they had beaten Ireland in a play-off for the European Nations Cup in Liverpool. Paddy was in the Kop, a famous terrace behind one of the goals at Anfield. The area is noted for spontaneous singing and it reverberated with the sound of Paddy's hit that evening. 'The Dutch had knocked us out of the competition. They did their lap of honour and came to the Kop, which was full of Irish fans. All the Irish crowd in the Kop sang "The Fields of Athenry" to the Dutch team and it was a very moving moment for me,' says Paddy.

Ireland's iconic soccer manager during that era was the late Jack Charlton. He too became friends with Paddy as 'The Fields of Athenry' was becoming an Irish anthem at soccer games around the globe.

'I knew Jack well – sure the two of us were on almost every TV show in the country during those times. The Irish team was flying; "The Fields of Athenry" was flying; and Jack and I became regulars on television shows. That's still an abiding memory for me,' says Paddy.

Paddy was at Giants Stadium in New Jersey in the USA in 1994, when the Irish soccer team beat Italy. 'The Fields of Athenry' was sung very loudly by the Irish crowd that day after Ray Houghton scored the winning goal.

'Oh yeah! That is an amazing memory, but the heat was so stifling! It was desperately warm that day for the spectators – what must it have been like for the players out there under that hot sun? I thought that the red-headed Steve Staunton was going to die out in the heat on the pitch. They all did well that day, but I thought Paul McGrath had probably the best game ever he had for Ireland. He was a great player and he's a lovely person as well,' says Paddy.

The trip to the USA in 1994 was slightly less eventful than an earlier trip to see Ireland play, during Italia '90. Back then, Paddy also travelled with former Irish football star the late Ray Treacy, of Ray Treacy Travel, along with 2,000 Irish fans. They travelled around Italy on a cruise liner to go to the matches! The reason for the cruise ship was that pubs and hotels on the mainland were not allowed to sell alcohol before the games. As one can imagine, this venture probably helped 'The Fields of Athenry' to gain an even stronger foothold with those Irish football fans, as they were singing it most nights on the ship.

'Well, we went on the *Achille Lauro* cruise ship, because everywhere was booked out. Another reason of course was because they had stopped serving drinks in Italian hotels before the games.

'So Ray Treacy hired seats on the *Achille Lauro*, and we all went on it. That caused any amount of problems regarding how those passengers were going to pay for their drink. On some of those cruises, you don't pay for anything at the time of purchase – you sign for everything and pay afterwards, before leaving the liner.

'But Ray Treacy found it hard to convince the cruise company that this system was not going to work with every one of the 2,000 Paddies on this boat! It wasn't a good idea asking them to sign their names for the drinks, and expecting them all to settle their bills afterwards. Of course, most would sign and pay later, but others were signing themselves as Georgie Best, Eusebio, Eamon Dunphy and Johnny Giles. Many of them were using fictitious names. So the cruise company had to get cash registers installed in the bar on the ship,' roars Paddy.

All was eventually sorted without attracting international headlines. But Paddy recalls many other moments when Irish sports fans on trips abroad made world media headlines – not for unpaid drinks, but for singing 'The Fields of Athenry'.

One such incident, from the Euros in 2012, continues to be recalled by newspapers, including the *Irish Post* in the UK. Writing in that paper in 2017, Aidan Lonergan recalled the moment when Irish voices were singing, even though Spain were beating them by four goals to nil.

'During the Euro 2012 group stage game against Spain, Irish fans started singing the song roughly eighty-three minutes into the game, and sang for the last six minutes, knowing that they were going to be knocked out. Some commentators stopped commenting for the final minutes, so the crowd could be heard. Recordings of the emotional event quickly went viral around the world.'

Pat Kehoe, on the website Ireland Calling, captured the event vividly:

'Football fans in most countries are a fickle bunch. When their team is losing they tend to scoff and jeer. Not the Irish. As their team were being outplayed on the pitch, the Irish fans raised their voices and began to sing their hearts out.

'Every time their team conceded another goal, the fans sang a little louder. Their chosen song was "The Fields of Athenry" – a story from the Great Famine about much greater hardship than could ever be found on a football field. On and on they sang until something wonderful happened – they became the story of the night. They outshone their team and they even outshone the brilliant Spanish team.'

The same website added that German TV was so impressed that the commentators stopped talking about the match so viewers could listen to the Irish fans uninterrupted. A Hungarian TV match commentator was so moved by it all, he said he was going to walk the three or four kilometres back to the city among the singing Irish fans.

In 2021, when the Irish rugby team had a historic win over the All Blacks in Dublin, the song that reverberated across the stadium, overshadowing the New Zealander's famous haka, was 'The Fields of Athenry'.

'Yeah, it was a great victory for the Irish. They sing the song at many of the rugby matches as well as at other sports events. It all started off in Parkhead with Glasgow Celtic, and Pete St John sang it there also. I'm delighted for Pete that they are still singing it, as he is a great guy,' says Paddy.

While Paddy was the singer who took the song to the masses worldwide, there was also a most unusual street performance of it on the streets of Athenry in 2019. On 6 May of that year, traditional musician Matt Cunningham from Galway, along with The Amazing Apples band and over 5,000 others, did a very different-style street performance of the song. Matt and 117 others played tin whistles as the crowd sang along and the iconic event was filmed for social media.

When Paddy was touring with The Dubliners, and later while dealing with health issues, he says he didn't follow the success of 'The Fields of Anfield Road' in the UK pop charts. It's an adaptation of the 'The Fields of Athenry', incorporating aspects of Liverpool's history. The song, credited to the Liverpool Collective featuring the Kop Choir, peaked at number fourteen in the UK pop charts in 2009. It was a number-one hit in Scotland that same year.

Paddy still has an interest in all versions of the song and in all sports, but mostly the GAA, rugby and soccer. Paddy and his son Ciarán are season ticket holders for Manchester United at Old Trafford. When it is suggested that they should be singing 'The Fields' there, Paddy replies, 'It would be more of a lament for them at the moment.'

Pete and Paddy have made the town of Athenry famous in many foreign fields, some that are very far flung from 'The Fields of Athenry'.

The man who penned Paddy's biggest hit, Pete St John, has spoken many times over the years about when he first realised it had hit potential. In an interview with Sean Creedon published in *Ireland's Own* in December 2020, Pete stated that he invited Paddy to a fund-raising concert in Washington DC, and hearing the song there may have influenced Paddy to record it. 'I got a call from Paddy Reilly who was working in New York at the time and I invited him down,' said Pete.

Pete and Paddy have many parallels in their lives, including both being true blue Dubliners from birth. Both spent substantial periods of their very different careers working in Canada and the US before returning to Dublin. While Paddy was singing in the States, Pete (who was born Peter Mooney) settled in Washington DC, where he worked in electrical engineering.

He wrote many songs, but when a singer named Jean Swift started singing his composition 'The Fields of Athenry' in folk clubs around Dublin, he says he first felt it had potential. In his 2020 interview with Sean Creedon, Pete said, 'I quickly realised that people jumped on the chorus and that maybe I had something special.'

This may have been almost a decade after it was written it before it became a hit. As London's *Irish Post* newspaper said in December 2021, 'The ballad was written in 1970 by prolific Irish composer Pete St John, whose other famous – yet slightly less well known – songs include The Rare Ould Times' and 'The Ferryman'.

Before emigrating to America, singer the late Danny Doyle had a hit in Ireland with another of Pete's songs, 'The Rare Ould Times', towards the end of 1979. As Pete recalled in 2020, 'Danny Doyle was a good friend of mine who emigrated to the US and got to hear 'The Fields' and decided to record it. It was fairly popular in the US.'

Pete added that Danny and Paddy were among the performers at a fund-raising concert in Washington DC at the Irish Inn, a pub managed by Pete's son Kieron. The concert featured songs that Pete had written, including 'The Fields of Athenry'.

'When Paddy Reilly went back to Ireland, he recorded the song and it went to number one in the charts and became a massive hit,' said Pete in 2020.

The song was described in that interview with Pete as 'the unofficial Irish sporting anthem'. It still is, even in post-COVID-19 Ireland, but perhaps sung in more subdued tones, according to COVID-19 expert Professor Luke O'Neill, writing in the *Irish Independent* in 2020.

'I was in the Aviva Stadium last Saturday to watch Ireland trounce Wales. It was great to see the stadium packed with fans again, all cheering Ireland on. But I noticed one thing. Not much singing. There was one attempt at "The Fields of Athenry", but it petered out.

'I might have been overthinking it, but I wondered if everyone was just feeling a little bit out of sorts because of what we've been through with COVID-19. A feeling of post-traumatic malaise?

If people say to Paddy Reilly that 'The Fields of Athenry' is an emigrant song or a sectarian song, they get this honest and curt reply: 'It's neither. It's a song about the Irish Famine and that's that.'

As Pete St John said in his interview with Sean Creedon, 'Some people may claim it's a sectarian song, but I don't think so; I wrote it about the Famine. There is a deep subliminal story behind the song. It's really the Holy Family again; it's the husband, wife and child; "Michael" is the Archangel.'

Irrespective of what message people take from the song, it has put Athenry (Baile Átha an Rí, Town of the Ford of the King) on the world stage. In olden times, some historians called Athenry Kingstown. In modern times, it is described on the Wikipedia website as 'also well known by virtue of the song "The Fields of Athenry"'.

Pete and Paddy have made the town famous in many foreign fields, some very farflung from 'The Fields of Athenry'. And Paddy's unique vocal timbre took 'The Fields of Athenry' into the stratosphere, beyond this world!

Paddy relates the strange story about how 'The Fields of Athenry' made it into outer space, a place where he has always wanted to go. An unfulfilled ambition of Paddy's was to go up in the space shuttle, as he said back in 1991 in an interview with Brian Carthy of RTÉ in his book *The A–Z of Country & Irish Stars*. When asked what his early ambitions were, Paddy replied that he wanted to be a doctor, but that 'my unfulfilled ambition is to go off on the space shuttle'.

'I would still love to go up there in the space shuttle,' says Paddy now, 'and if I got half a chance I would still go. My version of "The Fields of Athenry" was played in space during one of the US space missions.

'They used the song to waken up the astronauts. The pastor, or priest, for that flight crew was from Galway. He was saying some prayers with the astronauts before take-off, and he introduced them to the song. It was agreed that it should be used for their wake-up call, and so it was. That is how all that happened. I can't remember the name of the priest, but I'm glad that he did get me into space that way!

'It reminds me of a very witty remark, a real droll reply that one of my neighbours, Sean Keane of The Chieftains, made to another neighbour. The other neighbour, Henry, congratulated Sean about The Chieftains playing on the space shuttle. Sean in his own quiet way replied, "It was only a recording. We didn't go that far at all."'

* * *

Sadly, as this book was being researched and written, the songwriter Pete St John (AKA Peter Mooney), who was ninety, passed away in Dublin on 12 March 2022. Many of his friends and colleagues from the music business attended a ceremony of remembrance for him in Whitehall Church, Dublin, on Saturday, 2 April.

Pete's most famous composition was of course 'The Fields of Athenry'. It became an unofficial anthem for teams of many sports codes all over the world. In soccer it was used first by Glasgow Celtic FC, and later by Liverpool FC. GAA teams, the Irish national rugby and soccer teams and many others sing it, at venues from Athenry to Australia to the Arctic Circle and to Antarctica. As stated above, Paddy Reilly's hit version has even been played in outer space!

The passing of Pete engendered great sadness in the Co. Galway town immortalised in the vivid lyrics of his song. Athenry Heritage Centre manager Alan Burgess spoke of his many meetings with both Paddy Reilly and the late Pete. Alan praised both Pete and Paddy for bringing so many thousands of people from all over the world to the area due to the popularity of the song.

'Sometimes it would be individuals, couples, choirs, soccer and rugby teams and supporters.' Alan added that one of the first questions visitors ask is, 'Where are the fields of Athenry?' 'I reply that they are all around you. Once you come off the motorway, you can see all of Athenry and the fields surrounding it. You get a great perspective of it on arrival.'

Following his passing, Pete St John was also remembered on radio and TV programmes in Ireland and around the world. In west Australia, there was a huge reaction to a tribute programme presented on Perth's Radio Fremantle by former RTÉ producer Frank Murphy, who produced the Gay Byrne radio show on RTÉ for eighteen years.

Among the guests on the Perth radio tribute show was Fred Rea, the founder and publisher of the *Irish Scene* magazine in west Australia. Fred was a close friend of Pete St John over the years and an admirer of Paddy's version of the song.

Glen Hansard accompanies Paddy singing 'The Fields of Athenry' at the funeral of Pete St John.

Chapter 7

Paddy in the Lands Down Under

W hile Paddy still wants to travel into outer space in the space shuttle, he hated the long, slow aeroplane trips to and around Australia.

'I hated flying to Australia, but I loved playing there,' says Paddy. 'But to get there, you don't have any choice only to endure two flights that are each ten, twelve or fourteen hours long. Now I believe it can be done in one flight, but I'm sure that still means eighteen to twenty hours, including time spent at the airport.

'But travelling to and from Australia was all just part of my life, and it was still better than doing shift work at the Swiftbrook Paper Mills,' he laughs.

The fields, the concert halls, even some remote sheep-shearing stations across Australia opened up for shows by Paddy after the phenomenal success of 'The Fields of Athenry'. He did 'eight or nine' tours there, many of them along with the late Brendan Grace.

'The first time I went to Australia, it was as one of a number of Irish acts, including The Dubliners, Christy Moore, The Fureys, Brendan Grace and others. Jim Hand was on that tour.'

Playing in Sydney Opera House was a prestigious gig for Paddy during that tour. It was a memorable one for him, but he says it looks far bigger from the outside than it actually is inside.

'Don't get me wrong – it is a spectacular piece of architecture, but inside there are many halls and corridors, plus bars and restaurants, that take away from the size of the main concert hall.

'Of course, it was a highlight of my first trip to Australia with the Guinness Tour to get to play at Sydney Opera House. I enjoyed the experience immensely,' says Paddy.

Paddy talks fondly of his tours there with his friend Brendan Grace.

'Brendan was great to travel with. While some people could drive you crazy when travelling with them, he was different. Grace was a highly intelligent man. Many comedians can be boring, continuing to tell jokes when they are off the stage, but he wasn't like that at all.

'He would never, ever, tell a joke when travelling on those trips. When he was off stage, he was off stage, and that was it. It was goodbye to the stage work when he was off. Some performers never get off the stage even when they are travelling, and that can be annoying.'

Brendan recalled some funny incidents while touring with Paddy in Australia in his book *Amuzing Grace*, and he doesn't hide his admiration for Paddy's singing.

'Paddy Reilly is by far one of the best singers I know, but his escapades were even better and funnier again. He and I became a double act for years, touring Australia, America and Canada … Paddy was particularly big in Australia and he was a sure fire bet to bring in a large crowd as his records were constantly being played out there.'

While Paddy was popular in Australia, Brendan states in his book that he demanded equal applause as Paddy at one Australian concert! 'Paddy had recently sprained his wrist and playing a guitar at that gig was next to impossible for him. Fortunately, I knew all his chords and offered to play the guitar in the wing where I wouldn't be seen while he held his guitar and sang on stage, all the while pretending to strum the chords. To be honest, he needn't have bothered with the scheme because we ended up telling the crowd about it at the end of the show anyway. Paddy had received a standing ovation for his performance, so I walked out and demanded one as well for my guitar work. And with that the game was up.'

When they started touring abroad as a double act, Paddy and Brendan were both managed by Jim Hand. Paddy says that himself and Brendan Grace touring together in Australia was a very compatible arrangement. 'We were very together, we would decide before going on stage who would do the first half and who would close the show. There was never a problem – sometimes I would be up first; on other occasions I would do the second half.'

Some of the places they played in, especially in the more remote parts of Australia, were wool sheds, but they still had the most modern facilities. 'People would come from many miles around to the show in those places, and they were venues with first-class restaurants and modern bars. It might be a wool shed by name, but certainly not by nature.'

Getting to some of those venues could be difficult, because of the huge distances that they had to travel. Often going by plane from one place to another was the only option. But what happened when there was an airline strike?

'I remember being caught up in an airline strike while touring in Australia at one time, and I flew on everything except a kite to get to the gigs,' laughs Paddy. 'I even flew via crop dusters (tiny aircraft used to spray crops), and once on a private plane with gold fittings on the side of its seats, which was owned by some wealthy sultan.

'The crop duster planes were very different to that! So also were the times I travelled on the type of aircraft used by paratroopers, with just the side seats where you sit on a bench. You were strapped in, but the sides were open so you could jump out quickly. I flew on a few of them, and I think Brendan Grace was with me on one such flight, to take us to a gig in the outback. That must have been some sight!

'Australia is such a different country to tour – it's so vast and the distances you have to travel between gigs can be so great that it's unimaginable unless you've been there. After you get forty or fifty miles in from the coast in many parts of that vast continent, there is nothing but bush and desert. You can travel hundreds of miles and see nothing but kangaroos and other creatures of the wild before you come to the next outpost.

'We did lots of gigs in those towns in the middle of the bush, often in those vast sheep-shearing sheds. But we also played in places near the coast such as Wollongong, towns that often had fine, old-fashioned concert halls. Even though vast areas of that continent are so sparsely populated, we still did good crowds everywhere we went.

'Canada is similar in many parts. It's a huge country too, and I found many similarities in touring the two countries. Of course, Canada is so much colder, but in both places, the reality is that the climate doesn't permit people to live in many parts of them.'

While not all the people who travelled to Paddy's shows in Australia were of Irish or English descent, he doesn't think that any of the native aboriginals came to his concerts. 'Perhaps they did, but if so none of them came up to chat afterwards. I would like to have chatted with them, because they were treated very badly in the past, which still impacts on the present generations of aboriginals.

'I encountered some tragic examples of that in Sydney in particular, where, sadly, some of them were involved in heavy drinking and prostitution, especially in the King's Cross area.'

Some of the scenes there shocked and saddened Paddy, as he explains:

'We would often come back to Sydney late at night after playing somewhere out in the bush, and we'd go for a few drinks in the late-night bars around King's Cross. But some parts there, which were busy shopping areas like Dublin's Grafton Street during the day, were very different places after seven or eight in the evening.

'Some of those places became red-light areas, and so many of the young girls involved in prostitution there seemed to be aboriginals. Young girls – I can only describe it as horrific and heart-breaking.'

Brendan Grace had a similar view of parts of King's Cross in Sydney, as he says in his book *Amuzing Grace*:

'It was one of the most dreadful places I have ever been to. The devastation there at that time had to be seen to be believed. Drugs, crime, prostitution and homelessness were all major problems. I didn't realise it at the time but those problems had given it a worldwide reputation.'

Brendan also says in his book that when he came home, he told his kids to go there some day, just to experience the sadness he had seen there.

'I knew if they experienced it once it would scare the living daylights out of them as far as drugs were concerned.'

One time, after an arduous tour across the Australian outback, Paddy and Brendan were delighted to arrive in Adelaide to find a large table of Irish food laid out in front of them. Brendan said it was such a joy to sample Irish food again as they were approaching the end of a long tour of Australia where they ate mostly Australian or oriental foods. But Paddy says that 'Gracer never complained during that tour or any other tour of Australia about the different food we were served up – he just ate everything put in front of him. He'd even eat the cook as well'!

During the course of conversation with a lady named Kathleen, who had prepared the spread of Irish food for them in Adelaide, Brendan told her that one thing he and Paddy missed most from home was a Sunday Irish dinner. She offered to prepare a home-cooked Sunday dinner for the two of them in her house. 'A nice roast, cabbage, roast potatoes, Yorkshire pudding, the works,' recalled Brendan.

'The mouths of myself and Paddy were watering by the time she had finished telling us what she would prepare. We were to leave for Ireland that Sunday night, and so it would be the perfect send off. I think Paddy and I spent the night dreaming of this lunch because we had gone so long without a real Irish meal.'

On the appointed day, they had a few drinks before the taxi arrived to take them to their anticipated Sunday lunch.

The problem was, neither of them had asked Kathleen for her address!

'When we sat into the taxi, the driver asked us for the address of the house that we were going to. I turned to Paddy and said to tell him where we were going. Paddy replied, "Sure I don't know where we're effin' going Gracer." I thought Kathleen had given Paddy the address, while Paddy thought she had given it to me.'

Despite a series of frantic phone calls to other Irish people who might have had a number for Kathleen, and one to the Irish Club, which unfortunately was closed that day, they failed to find the address for her.

'We ended up drowning our sorrows in the hotel bar that day,' recalls Paddy. 'Gracer remembered the incident in far greater detail than I did. After getting back to Ireland, he phoned the Irish Club again and got Kathleen's address from somebody there. He wrote to her to apologise for our no-show at her home.'

Paddy loved playing in Perth, and he also loved the countryside around this part of west Australia. 'If I was to live anywhere in Australia, I would live in Perth,' he says. 'It's such a beautiful city on the Swan River. I also loved going out to Fremantle, where the yachts once took part in the Americas Cup.'

This famous yacht race was held in Fremantle in 1987, the first time in its 123-year history that it was held anywhere outside America. It resulted in massive international interest in Perth, Fremantle and west Australia as a whole. The boost it gave to tourism is still visible in Perth and Fremantle to this day. It resulted in huge investment in the infrastructure of the port and all of the seaside area around Fremantle.

Paddy and his songs, especially his iconic rendition of 'The Fields of Athenry', still resonate with people who emigrated to Perth a lifetime ago, and with some of the new young Irish there as well. One of the biggest admirers of the talents of both Paddy Reilly and Pete St John is veteran Perth magazine publisher Fred Rea. Rea is also a musician, and an emigrant to that city from Cork over fifty years ago.

He has often written in laudatory terms about Paddy's singing of 'The Fields of Athenry' during his time as managing editor and publisher of the *Irish Scene*, a Perth-based magazine. The publication is regarded as a bible for the Irish and their descendants in west Australia over the last twenty-five years.

Fred Rea states that, in his opinion, 'The Fields of Athenry' has done as much for Irish music and culture around the world as 'Riverdance'.

'In three verses, plus the chorus, that song, telling the tale of "Michael" being deported to the other end of the world from his wife "Mary", during the Famine, resonates with Irish people everywhere. The characters in that song may be fictional, but it's so brilliantly written by Pete St John, and sung by Paddy Reilly, that it's a microcosm of what really happened in Ireland in Famine times.

'Possibly every hour of the day, and definitely every day of the year, somewhere in the world somebody Irish, or of Irish ancestry, is either singing or listening to that song on radio or some other media platform. Forget about "Danny Boy" – "The Fields of Athenry" is a far more moving song, especially when sung by Paddy Reilly,' says Fred.

'Paddy sings it in a key that is neither too high nor too low, but just right for other people to sing along with him. His key when singing "The Fields of Athenry" was also the key, in another sense of the word, to making his version so successful.'

Given that his fans in west Australia were so welcoming when he toured there over the years, it's no great surprise that Paddy Reilly says that Perth is one of his favourite cities in the world. 'Perth is a gorgeous city, and it's so civilised. There are so many people of Irish descent there', he says.

Paddy adds that the audiences in the Australian outback were also hugely enthusiastic, as was the crowd at the prestigious Melbourne Concert Hall, where he played to an audience of 5,000 people.

While playing to 5,000 fans in Melbourne remains one of the highlights for Paddy from his tours of Australia, that show started out as one where tickets were slow to sell. Linking up with former Dublin footballer Jim Stynes, then a big star with Melbourne Australian Football Club, was the key to selling out all the tickets for his concert in the Melbourne Concert Hall.

Jim Stynes left Dublin as an eighteen-year-old to play Australian Football League (AFL) in Melbourne where he became one of the biggest stars in AFL.

'I remember the late Jim Stynes being a big hero in Melbourne at a time when tickets for my Melbourne show were slow to sell. I was in Sydney and the promoter asked if I had known Jim Stynes back in Dublin and I said yes. He then got to work on some extra publicity for the gig and had me fly to Melbourne to get my picture taken with Jim. Before going to Australia, while still a teenager, Jim had played Gaelic football with Ballyboden St Enda's, and he won a Minor All-Ireland with Dublin when he was growing up.

'The promoter said I would need to go to Melbourne the very next morning to have my picture taken with him for the newspapers. I took an early-morning flight from Sydney to Melbourne and got a picture taken with him, and we had lunch together. It was on the front page of the main daily newspaper there the next day, and the show sold out overnight. He was a legend in Australian Football,' says Paddy.

Sadly, Jim Stynes died from cancer at the age of forty-five in 2012, after a three-year battle with the disease. 'I believe that his funeral was one of the biggest ever seen in Melbourne. He was a true gentleman, and I'm so glad to have met him in Melbourne,' adds Paddy.

Melbourne holds a special place in Paddy's heart also for another reason, and that is because of his love of horse racing. He doesn't hide his is admiration for the success down under of Irish father and son racing trainers Aidan and Joseph O'Brien.

'I'd love to be back there for the Melbourne Cup or the Cox Plate. Young O'Brien (Joseph O'Brien) won the Cox Plate and the Melbourne Cup. He was only in his twenties when he won both. He was following in the footsteps of his father Aidan O'Brien, who had the big winner in Australian racing with Adelaide back in 2014.'

'Yes, Australia was a good place to tour,' says Paddy. 'But it could be a demanding schedule too – we might be on breakfast television shows almost every morning, like at 6.30 or 7am, because there were no daily papers in the bush. So while concerts in Sydney, Melbourne or Perth were easy to advertise in newspapers, there was no such way of advertising shows in the remote parts. TV, or in some instances radio, was the only way of getting our concerts in the more remote areas publicised. This was long before all this social media stuff came along!'

When touring Australia with Brendan Grace, they would synchronise their early-morning TV appearances. Paddy would go on one channel and Brendan would go on the other, 'so that way we got the best of both worlds', says Paddy.

While 'The Fields of Athenry' was the big song for Paddy among TV viewers, radio listeners and buyers of Irish records in Australia, Australian TV presenters also focussed on other songs that he sang. 'Yeah, they had TV shows to fill – while they were interested in the story about the man from Athenry being deported to Botany Bay, they wanted to know about other Irish songs too. They were all very professional in their approach, and they didn't just concentrate on one song,' says Paddy.

Paddy says that the boredom of the long plane journeys to and from Australia would be the biggest deterrent to him ever going there again. 'People sometimes ask me, how can you get rid of a fear of flying? And I reply, just fly to Australia – you will be hoping the feckin' plane would crash so you could get off it. After that, short flights of a few hours will never worry you again,' he laughs.

'The boredom was shocking. Even if we stopped off in places such as Dubai or Abu Dhabi, it was still a gruelling trip.'

On one of those long, boring flights to Australia, the late John Hurt, famous for his film roles in *A Man For All Seasons* and *The Elephant Man*, asked if he could sit beside Paddy and his manager Jim Hand.

Asked if he and Jim Hand got on well with John Hurt during that flight, Paddy replies, 'You don't have much choice when you're stuck on an airplane for twelve or fourteen hours, or whatever length the flight was! Only joking; John Hurt was a nice man. We were all travelling business class. He came up to us and said something like, "Ye seem like a right pair of arseholes; do ye mind if I join ye?" I think he was off the drink at that time, but we had good craic with him while Jim and I were drinking our way to Sydney.'

Paddy says that during those long plane trips, he often thought about how sad it must have been for people such as 'Michael' in the song 'The Fields of Athenry', who would have spent weeks or months on a ship getting there. 'At that time it must have been like going to a prison at the other end of the Earth for our people who were sent out there, and for people deported from England also.'

But there were lighter moments too. 'I remember a story that somebody in Australia told me, during one of our trips, about an English chap being held for questioning after arrival in Sydney or Perth,' says Paddy. 'The Australian immigrations officer – and some of them can be very strict – said to him, "Have you a prison record?" to which the Englishman replied, "Oh dear, is it still necessary to have one to get in here?"'

Paddy says that while most Irish people who emigrated to Australia over the decades seem to love living there, there is a cohort of emigrants who want to come back but can't. 'Some people I met out there were sad because they couldn't return to live again in Ireland, as they had hoped when they went there first. After getting work in Australia, they may have got married and had children, and when those children reached a certain age, thirteen or fourteen or so, they didn't want to come to live in Ireland.

'In a few cases, parents I met there told me that while they could afford to come back to Ireland, they can't, because all of their family are Australian. On the other hand, there are many who wouldn't want to come back to our cold weather anyway,' he laughs.

Paddy pays tribute to the great Irish communities that are in most Australian cities, as he also evidenced in other places around the world where the Irish settled. 'The Irish have always been great for circling the wagons, so to speak, looking after each other no matter where they are abroad. Sometimes even better than back at home.

'I remember some American saying to me that "it must be so goddamn awful awkward" for me being back home – not being able to enjoy a drink without people coming up to me for autographs, welcoming me back and chatting. But I replied that sometimes when I go into my local pub back home, after an American tour, there might be five or six at the bar who would mutter under their breaths, "This bollix is back from America again," and we would all laugh about it. That's the other side of the coin,' roars Paddy.

Paddy would have loved to play for the Irish, and those of Irish descent, in New Zealand, but that never happened. 'I never got to play in New Zealand, because it seems that one of our promoters in Australia had problems getting paid for a tour that other Irish acts were on when he was promoting them there.

'When the opportunity arose for me to play some shows in New Zealand, he wanted the money upfront before sending me to do any shows there. They didn't come up with the money in advance, and so I never got to play there'.

Paddy did, however, get to play in Hong Kong. 'I played at the opening of a bar in Hong Kong on my way to do one of the Australian tours,' he recalls. 'That came about through champion Irish jockey Mick Kinane, who was also a champion jockey in Hong Kong for years.'

When Mick Kinane retired in 2009, the *Guardian* newspaper described him as 'the world-class jockey who knew no boundaries … Kinane would go anywhere to take on the locals on their own turf and terms and frequently hand them a lesson in horsemanship.'

Mick's friendship with Paddy knew no boundaries either, and he was responsible for him playing in Hong Kong. 'Mick was living there at the time, and I stayed with him and his wife Catherine, who were very good to me. We had great times at the races there – Mick Kinane was treated like a king over there.

'I did a full two-hour show in Hong Kong, and got a good reaction from the Irish and all others at the gig as well. Hong Kong is a unique place really, because, while it has a huge population, very few of them are natives of the city.

'I enjoyed Hong Kong; I found that it was the only place in the world where they move faster than New York. If you walk down a street in New York and a tailor threw a measuring tape on you for making a new suit, he might have it ready for you to wear a few hours later! Hong Kong is a bit like that.'

Paddy loved attending race meetings at the two major race courses in Hong Kong. 'They race there several days a week on those two courses – Happy Valley and the Sha Tin Racecourse. The latter one is the bigger; it can hold about 80,000 spectators.

'The people in Hong Kong love their races. I think that almost everybody there must gamble on something or other; it's unbelievable. Shop assistants would sometimes be on their mobile phones backing horses while they served you.'

On one occasion in Australia, Paddy met up with one of his favourite songwriters – Eric Bogle, who was born in Scotland but emigrated to Australia at the age of twenty-five. Eric wrote many famous folk songs, and two of the best-known are anti-war songs. One of these, 'And the Band Played Waltzing Matilda', was a massive hit for Paddy's friend Liam Clancy.

The song is about a young Australian soldier who comes back from the First World War badly maimed after the Battle of Gallipoli. He was fighting for the Allied forces in a division of the Australian and New Zealand Army Corps (ANZAC). Sadly, he came back without his legs, which were blown off by 'a big Turkish shell'. Back home in Australia, he and those around him wonder what they were fighting for, so far away from their homeland. Eric got into some controversy initially over this song, because some people thought it was anti-ANZAC.

Another big hit written by Eric Bogle is also about the First World War. 'The Green Fields of France' was taken into the higher echelons of the UK pop charts by The Furey Brothers and Davy Arthur.

'They are both powerful songs about the woeful waste of life in war,' says Paddy. '"And the Band Played Waltzing Matilda" wasn't an anti-ANZAC song at all. It about people going to their deaths for nothing, for no reason. It's a marvellous song. Eric wrote so many great songs; he is a genius as a songwriter, and I was so delighted to meet up with him and spend time with him in Australia.

'Eric came to a few of my gigs, and he brought me to his house on some nights off for dinner. We talked about both of our lives on the road as entertainers and about songs in general. Eric is a good Scotsman and he likes his Scotch whisky, as I do. So, in honour of us getting together in Australia during those few nights, we killed off a bottle of Scotch *each*,' recalls Paddy.

Chapter 8

The Dubliners Years

For Paddy Reilly, becoming a full-fledged member of the globally famous The Dubliners must have been the achievement of a lifetime, but he is fairly nonchalant about it.

'Sure I was always first or second sub on their team anyway, any time one of the members was missing,' he says.

The Dubliners held him in high regard from the early days. Back then, as a fan, the same age as themselves, he would get up to sing a few songs with them on stage at The Embankment in Tallaght. John Sheahan of The Dubliners says they knew immediately when they heard him sing that Paddy had a vocal talent that was special and different. He says they all realised from the first time hearing his voice how unique Paddy sounded compared to other fans who would get up on stage to sing with them.

Even when he became a full member of the group, Paddy looked different

The Dubliners in 1996 (left to right): Seán Cannon, Eamonn Campbell, Barney McKenna, John Sheahan and Paddy Reilly.

to the rest of The Dubliners. When asked why he wouldn't conform to their stage image as bearded balladeers, Paddy gives a very curt reply: 'Some singers have beards, and others don't. It makes no difference to their singing if they have a beard or not. When I joined The Dubliners and people asked if I was going to grow a beard, my reply was that I didn't need a beard to sing.'

His decision to join the group made news headlines on RTÉ TV in 1996. The headline on the national TV screens read that 'Folk singer and guitarist Paddy Reilly, best known for his 1984 hit "The Fields of Athenry", has taken on the role of full-time lead vocalist with The Dubliners.'

Newsreader and RTÉ Arts Correspondent Colm Connolly, himself a former singer with The Paramount Showband back in the 1960s, presented the story for the main evening news. He asked Paddy why he was giving up a successful solo career to join The Dubliners.

'I figure that at fifty-six, I was due a career change,' Paddy responded with a loud guffaw of a laugh.

Connolly's report continued that at the Baggot Inn on Merrion Row, The Dubliners launched *Further Along*, their first album featuring Paddy Reilly on lead vocals. 'He joins band members Barney McKenna on banjo, fiddle player John Sheahan, guitarists Eamonn Campbell and Seán Cannon. Having spent much of the previous decade in America, he is relishing the prospect of touring in Europe with The Dubliners.'

The RTÉ news report added that John Sheahan of the group offered some advice to the new band member: 'Paddy should take everything with moderation!'

Colm Connolly noted that among those attending the album launch was Ronnie Drew, who was still great friends with the band members. 'There's no unsolved rows or anything; everything is grand and I'm delighted to see the lads touring and I hope they keep her going,' said Ronnie.

The Dubliners album on which Paddy made his debut as lead singer was a big success. The sleeve notes echoed the sentiments of the RTÉ report about the smooth passing on of the baton of lead singer from Ronnie to Paddy:

'*Further Along* is a significant milestone in the long and colourful career of The Dubliners. It marks the departure of Ronnie Drew after 34 years and the arrival of Paddy Reilly, Ireland's best loved ballad singer. He is a long-time friend who has guested with them both on record and on stage on numerous occasions.'

Paddy's influence is apparent from the first song on the album, as he belts out a song that is very much associated with him – the Sean McCarthy composition 'Step It Out Mary'. The vocals on the *Further Along* also feature Sean Cannon, with Cannon singing the only Irish-language track, 'Tá an Coileach ag Fógairt an Lae'. 'Sean is a good linguist and he was well able to sing that song, and many others in Irish. He was big into languages,' says Paddy.

'The decision to put songs that I had recorded, such as "Cavan Girl", "Working Man", "The Craic Was Ninety in the Isle of Man", "The Coming of the Road" and others, was to add some of my songs to theirs. It was putting a bit of me into The Dubliners. But I have no clue regarding who came up with the idea to put a didgeridoo onto the intro of "Working Man". It must be someone in the recording studio – it certainly wasn't me anyway,' laughs Paddy.

Paddy loves Barney's version of the instrumental 'Ar Éireann Ní Neosfainn Cé Hí' on the album. 'It is so lovely the way he played that on the banjo. Barney was a genius,' he says.

When Paddy joined the Dubliners to replace Ronnie Drew, it was the second time that Ronnie had left the group. He departed from The Dubliners first in 1973, to spend more time with his family, and was replaced then by Jim McCann, another great friend of Paddy and of The Dubliners. Jim remained with them until 1979, and then went on to pursue a solo career. He had a massive hit with the song 'Grace', also recorded in recent years by Rod Stewart.

Ronnie rejoined The Dubliners in '79 and remained a member until 1995, when he left to work as a solo artist and was replaced by Paddy. But both of them performed together in The Dubliners for a number of reunion concerts and TV appearances, including The Dubliners' fortieth anniversary concert in 2002. One notable TV clip, still popular on social media channels, has Paddy singing his rousing version of 'The Craic Was Ninety in the Isle of Man', with Ronnie joining him in the chorus.

Ronnie was one of the original founders of the outfit, along with Luke Kelly. The Dubliners began in 1962 as The Ronnie Drew Ballad Group, in O'Donoghue's Bar on Merrion Row in Dublin. However, Ronnie didn't like the name. When he saw Luke reading James Joyce's *Dubliners*, it was the catalyst for a famous name change for the group.

Paddy Reilly was among their first fans, and was a regular in their audiences. So becoming a full-fledged member of The Dubliners in 1996, after being 'a sub' on the team many times, was never going to be a major sea change in the life of Paddy Reilly. He had already featured on their *25 Years Celebration* album, along with other guest singers like Christy Moore and the aforementioned Jim McCann.

'Ronnie Drew had had enough of the road by 1995,' says Paddy. 'He hated the travelling – as we all did, but Ronnie hated it more than the rest of us. So he got out and I went in when he left, at John Sheahan's invitation. I had a personal relationship with Ronnie and Luke, as well as with Jim McCann. We were all related through drink,' he says with a laugh.

'Jim and I were on the same bill in The Old Shieling Hotel for four or five years, and we both worked solo as well as with The Dubliners, so we were all friends on the same scene.'

Sadly, so many of Paddy's great friends from younger times with The Dubliners, including Ronnie Drew, Jim McCann, Luke Kelly, Barney McKenna, Eamonn Campbell, and from much earlier Ciarán Bourke, passed away long before their time.

Ciarán Bourke was the first to depart this life, at only fifty-three years of age. He was a founding member of The Dubliners, but had to leave the band after suffering a brain aneurism while touring with them in the UK. He was operated on in a London hospital, and later recuperated in Dublin. Bourke rejoined the group again for a short time, but was forced to quit for a second time while on a European tour with them.

Back in 1962, he was one of the founding four members of the group, and he toured with them extensively until his illness in 1974. A fluent Irish speaker, Ciarán Bourke translated many of the group's ballads from Irish into English.

Though paralysed and in a wheelchair, Ciarán performed a verse of 'Lament for Brendan Behan' from the audience on his last 'Late Late Show'

TV appearance. He sang in a clear, powerful and passionate voice after being invited to do so by host Gay Byrne. Afterwards, as John Sheahan played the fiddle intro to 'The Auld Triangle', the cameras panned to the audience as Ciarán sang along with the rest of the group and guests, who included Taoiseach Charlie Haughey.

'I missed out on that show, as I was away in San Francisco at that time doing some solo shows,' says Paddy.

Sadly, Ciarán Bourke passed away the next year, in May 1988. Though Paddy wasn't a regular member of the group during the years that Ciarán was with them, he still knew him well.

'Yeah, Ciarán got brain haemorrhages so young, and he couldn't walk towards the end of his life, couldn't do anything much for himself. It was so sad. I knew Ciarán from the early days of The Dubliners in Howth, and he was so talented. But like many on our scene, he was hard on himself too,' says Paddy.

Of course, Luke Kelly was a pal of Paddy's from the early days of the group. While Paddy worked with him intermittently in the group, Luke had passed on when he became a full-time member in 1996.

'I knew Luke from the days they started playing in O'Donoghue's pub and in the hotel in Howth, and he encouraged me in my interest in the songs of Ewan McColl. Luke was singing in the workingmen's clubs in England in those early days with McColl. He would bring back songs by McColl to me and to other singers like me. I never met McColl, but the songs he wrote were brilliant.'

Paddy recorded a full album of Ewan McColl songs, though he is very honest in saying that it wasn't a commercial success. He included one of the classic McColl songs, 'Dirty Old Town', as a track on his debut album with The Dubliners in 1996.

Paddy's great friendship with Luke and the rest of The Dubliners never diminished over the decades. 'The Dubliners were friends of mine since I was in my twenties, Luke especially. He and I were very good pals. We used to play a lot of golf together. It was always great to go golfing with Luke, because it was a toss-up regarding which of us was the worst. But Luke thought that he was as good as Arnold Palmer,' laughs Paddy.

Luke Kelly also passed away all too young, at the age of only forty-four in January 1984. His passing made the top of the front page of the *Irish Press* newspaper, then one of Ireland's biggest-selling daily papers. The newspaper tribute to Luke mentioned other jobs that he had worked in England as well as singing, including working as a vacuum cleaner sales-man, a hotel cellerman and a window cleaner.

Among those at his bedside when he died in 1984 were Ronnie Drew and newer member of The Dubliners at that time Eamonn Campbell.

In the *Irish Press* story, Eamonn said that due to his illness, Luke's role in the group had been hampered in the years leading up to his death, while Eamonn's own part became more prominent. He added that they had developed a strong and deep friendship.

Ronnie Drew passed away after a long illness in 2008, aged seventy-three. The *Irish Times* reported on how iconic he was as a singer of Irish ballads.

'Drew, originally from Dún Laoghaire, had been an iconic figure on the traditional music scene in Ireland for over five decades.

'He founded the then-Ronnie Drew Group in 1962, which later came to be known as The Dubliners.

'They emerged from back-room sessions in O'Donoghues pub in Dublin to become world-renowned.

'Drew sang one of the band's biggest commercial hits, when they entered the UK top ten in 1967 with "Seven Drunken Nights" and appeared on the BBC's "Top of the Pops".

'In 1995 they appeared again on the show with Shane McGowan and The Pogues, who performed with Drew on their single "The Irish Rover".'

Paddy speaks fondly of his friendship with Ronnie. 'Even after I joined The Dubliners, when he left, we kept in touch. We made a number of appearances singing together, some for TV shows to celebrate anniversaries of the founding of the group.'

Banjo Barney McKenna from Donnycarney in north Dublin is another member of The Dubliners who was a lifelong friend of Paddy and who has also gone to his eternal reward. During his nine-year stint with the group, Paddy remembers Barney as a really witty man with a dry sense of humour.

'Barney would come out with some great one-liners when we were touring together. I remember a great one that he came out with when we arrived at an airport in Berlin for a German tour. There were a lot of young airport attendants helping us when we were collecting our luggage and Barney quipped, "These kids are fierce intelligent, and they're all speaking German." Yeah, Barney had a great sense of humour.'

Barney was the last of the founding members of The Dubliners. He died in April 2012, at the age of seventy-two. It shows the stature of The Dubliners internationally that when Barney died, the influential UK newspaper the *Guardian* published a lengthy tribute to him. It featured a photo of Barney and the previously deceased Ronnie Drew in a jovial mood, singing at a street corner. Paddy Reilly says that Barney's sudden death came as a terrible shock to him. They had been working together until a few years earlier, and the banjo maestro never seemed to grow old.

Reminiscing while leafing through old black-and-white photographs of the early line-up of The Dubliners in his Rathcoole home, Paddy becomes melancholy talking about them. 'So many of them have gone, and all too young. It was a hard life touring around the world. It took its toll, as did the drinking and the cigarettes,' he sighs.

Another member of The Dubliners during Paddy's tenure with the group was the late Eamonn Campbell. But he was more than just a touring colleague, as he also produced or else played on most of Paddy's solo albums.

Eamonn Campbell took ill while doing what he loved best, touring with a folk group. That's according to a report on the RTÉ TV main evening news in October 2017. He was seventy.

'Campbell fell ill late last week while touring with The Dublin Legends in the Netherlands and Belgium, a statement from his family said. He died on Wednesday night (18 October), surrounded by his family. The news of his death was announced by The Dublin Legends Facebook page, a group Campbell formed with fellow surviving members of The Dubliners after the veteran folk balladeers retired in 2012.'

A report in the *Irish Independent* on the large attendance at the funeral of Eamonn in 2017 stated that Eddie Furey, Seán Cannon and Paddy Reilly helped to carry the remains of Dubliner Eamonn Campbell from St Agnes Church, Crumlin, watched by celebrant Father Brian D'Arcy. It also featured a photo of Paddy and his music friends carrying the wicker coffin with Eamonn's remains to the waiting hearse.

It was further proof of how well-loved all The Dubliners were and are, and their longevity in the memory of the media and the general public.

'Eamonn was such a brilliant musician and an equally talented record producer. Along with John Sheahan, they worked on most of the albums that I did,' says Paddy. His close association with those two men in record-ing studios over the years made joining The Dubliners on the road all the easier for him.

'It made it so easy when we went touring together, as we didn't have to do any rehearsing. During my years with The Dubliners, we could go straight out on stage and start playing, as we knew each other so well. We knew what we were supposed to do for the live shows – or at least we pro-fessed to know anyway,' says Paddy with a loud laugh.

'It was a smooth transition for me to join The Dubliners. I was always a bit nervous before going on stage as a solo artist. But if I thought I'd be less nervous with the rest of The Dubliners around me, I was wrong. However, they were all so supportive of me, and even described me as the "new kid on the block" during my first German tour with them.'

On that tour, John Sheahan introduced Paddy to the German audiences more or less as the youngster in the group! That humorous introduction is captured on the live album that The Dubliners did while touring in Ger-many, titled *Alive-Alive-O*.

If John's introduction of Paddy to the crowd was a bit tongue-in-cheek, Paddy's explanation to the Germans of the story behind 'Step It Out Mary' was equally humorous: 'This song was written all about matchmaking, and if ye are not familiar with the term, it refers to a time in Ireland years and years ago, when men didn't like to get married too young. So the match-maker went around the country and he got young ladies of eighteen to twenty years old, and he matched them up as suitable to marry young men who were only sixty-eight or seventy years old!

'The match was usually made with those good, nice, wild young fellows. But the young lady always need to have fifty or sixty acres of good bog (peat) land for her dowry (money or property given to the husband in marriage). The reasoning behind all this was because her family thought that the young bride would get the old groom into the marriage bed and kill him off in the first week. But these old guys lived on until they were about 110, because they were so fit from running around chasing livestock.

'Suddenly, the young woman was middle-aged after having twenty-three children, and the man would be in the pub until two or three in the morning, drinking twenty-five pints of Guinness. Then, even when he was 104 or more, he would come home in the early hours of the morning, full of the joys of spring and looking for more action. Oh, the mind plays great tricks on some people after they had drank twenty-five pints of Guinness,' said Paddy to roars of laughter from the German audience.

The album is a mix of songs and tunes representative of The Dubliners' repertoire at that time, including songs from the repertoire of Paddy Reilly. Naturally, his iconic hit 'The Fields of Athenry' was met with rapturous applause from German audiences.

Sean Cannon shared singing duties with Paddy on most of the tracks, with John Sheahan doing most of the introductions as well as playing some fiddle solos. The atmosphere of that German tour was captured very well on the double album *Alive-Alive-O*, released on the Baycourt label in 1997.

Paddy says he loved his times touring with The Dubliners, saying that the group was particularly popular in Austria, Switzerland and Germany.

'They were as big as The Beatles in Germany. I remember one night when we did a concert in the Convention Centre in Hamburg, and the Mayor of the city came on stage to make a special presentation to The Dubliners.

'They were the only group ever to sell out the Convention Centre in Hamburg thirty-five years on the trot. While I was with them there in the latter years, they had been doing this for thirty years before I ever joined them in Germany. I also loved touring with them in Austria, Slovenia and Croatia.

'There was no language barrier at any of those concerts, as the audiences all had a good knowledge of English. Maybe in one or two places in Germany there was a slight language barrier, but in most places, and especially in Austria and Holland, all those at the shows knew English.'

Paddy also has great memories of touring in Denmark and the Scandinavian countries, but one memory that stands out above all others is playing at the massive international Tonder Folk Festival in Denmark.

The Tonder festival is held for several days and nights every August since 1975. It takes place in an arena that can hold 15,000 fans and features mostly international folk, country and roots music acts. Some of those that have appeared there include Steve Earle, The Red Hot Chilli Peppers, The Mavericks, Emmylou Harris and from Ireland The Dubliners, The Chieftains and Mary Black, as well as UK pop star of the 1960s Donovan, who Paddy was delighted to meet.

One of the reasons that he was happy to meet Donovan was because the first song Paddy played on the guitar was the UK singer's hit 'Yellow is the Colour' when he got his first guitar at twenty-three.

'I was playing with The Dubliners when they were top of the bill at one of the festivals in Tonder. Donovan was also on the show, and I was delighted to have a drink and a chat with him backstage. I asked him, how the hell did he get to go to India with The Beatles when they toured there? He told me the reason he got to go with them was because he could fingerpick on the guitar, and John Lennon couldn't do so at that time.

'Imagine that – The Beatles brought Donovan with them to India to teach John how to fingerpick on the guitar. Being rock musicians, they would be more used to using a plectrum on the guitar. Donovan was a gentleman to chat with, and our meeting in Denmark also gave me the opportunity to tell him how much I loved his song 'Yellow is the Colour' when I was starting out singing and playing in Dublin. There the two of us were, decades later, talking about it backstage at one of the biggest folk festivals in Europe.'

The Tonder festival is a prestigious event to perform at, but, like many other major outdoor festivals, it is not as glamorous for the artists as fans might imagine. 'While the Tonder festival probably attracts over 100,000 people, it can be hard to get accommodation for many of them,' says Paddy. 'Some might have nowhere booked to stay, and they might be sleeping on floors in schools and halls. I remember when we were there, we were unlucky, as it rained for the whole weekend.

'There must be about 30,000 people in one camp site, with mud and water everywhere. I remember one very funny incident when we were leaving and the coaches were picking us up from houses and schools where we were staying. We were wet and cold and sleepless, but we all burst into laughter at one such stop where we collected American singer-songwriter Tom Paxton. He got on the coach at about five o'clock in the morning. We were all wrecked. We were being taken to the airport to get on planes to take us to our respective homes, longing to get to a warm bed. Then Paxton gets on the coach, tired like the rest of us, and he shouts, "Good morning, folks; we wouldn't be in this business only for the glamour!" Even though we were all ringing wet, hungry and cold, what could we do but laugh? That's the other side of the touring that nobody sees – getting back to airports from gigs and maybe six or seven hours on a bus with little or no heat, which happens in many places.'

But memories of wet, weary, long journeys blur into nothingness when Paddy remembers the joy of performing to enthusiastic fans on so many shows with The Dubliners, including their fortieth anniversary concert at Dublin's Gaiety theatre.

'That was a great one, but, like lots of things that we did in the group, the words "preparation" and "Dubliners" didn't always go together. But the show was put together by promoter Pat Egan. He is a gentleman, and he did a great job of making it all such a memorable production.'

On that concert, Paddy launched into a stirring version of the 1916 rebel song 'The Foggy Dew', very similar to the way he sang it on the *Alive-Alive-O* album. The fiddle sounds of John Sheahan also provided a suitable intro for Paddy's rendition of his hit 'The Town I Loved So Well' on the Gaiety show.

He got a standing ovation from every tier of the capacity attendance at the Gaiety that night when he sang 'Molly Malone' without his hallmark guitar strung over his shoulder. This gave Paddy greater freedom as he raised his hands to encourage the audience to sing along. They reacted with enthusiasm to his encouragement, as the thousands in the audience raised the roof singing along with him.

Ronnie was there on stage that night, as were Jim McCann and Sean Cannon. The less-inclined-to-sing members of The Dubliners, John Sheahan and Barney McKenna, set aside their instruments and for a time they sang along too.

'We also did the Legends of Folk show with Ronnie and The Dubliners, Liam Clancy and Finbar Furey and others. That was great fun.' The tin whistle playing of John Sheahan on 'The Fields of Athenry', as Paddy sang his greatest hit, added extra poignancy to the live version of the song on that show.

While The Dubliners were huge in the UK and all across Europe, they found it harder to make a similar impression in America. That might go back to the early days of the folk and ballad boom there, when The Clancy Brothers and Tommy Makem lorded over it all on that side of the Atlantic, while The Dubliners did likewise on this side of the big pond. Paddy says that while The Dubliners always did well enough in the USA, there was less euphoria about them there than in Europe.

'It's hard to know why The Dubliners didn't become massive in America, notwithstanding that they always had a substantial following there. It might have been something to do with a certain conservativeness that manifests itself in some Americans. The hair and beards of The Dubliners, when they went over there first, might not have gone down well with some in the USA. It was at a time when many young Americans were in the army service overseas, with heads almost shaved. It's hard to know, but maybe, just maybe, that might have been a reason, because The Dubliners did so well on the "Ed Sullivan Show" the first time they went there.

'I will always remember the first time I was in New York. When I went to the top of the Empire State Building, the first thing I saw, looking out across the city, was a huge billboard of The Dubliners. They stood out in that picture because of their big beards, and they had so much hair. At that time many young men in America had tight hair, and it symbolised their army duty. The Dubliners looked very different! I didn't get to see or meet them in America back then; it was decades later that I joined them.'

Paddy left The Dubliners in 2005. He was diagnosed with cancer a few months later, a few days after finishing the show 'The Legends of Irish Folk', which ran at the Gaiety theatre and later in Vicar Street. The show featured Liam Clancy, Ronnie Drew and Finbar Furey. Patsy was replaced by Patsy Watchorn of The Dublin City Ramblers.

'Yeah, Patsy went into The Dubliners after I moved on. I knew him for years, from The Dublin City Ramblers. Sure, we were all friends from working on the music circuit together for most of our lives,' says Paddy.

He says his years with The Dubliners were 'great times and fun times'. He felt honoured to be invited to join them after being 'on the subs bench' for so long!

At the Áras at a Tribute to The Dubliners night, 2015. (right to left:) Ciaran Reilly, Sabina Higgins, Paddy Reilly, Michael D Higgins, Jean Berns and Ashling Reilly.

Chapter 9

Paddy Through the Eyes of Others

There is a certain mystique about singers, actors and other performers in the eyes of fans who see them on stage or screen or hear them on records. To find out more about Paddy when growing up, or away from the spotlights, or working with colleagues on stage or in studios, we spoke to family members, friends and work colleagues.

John Sheahan of The Dubliners has known Paddy for decades, as has musician, singer-songwriter and producer Phil Coulter. Paddy's son Ciarán is more than just a family member; he is a close confidant, companion at race meetings and business associate. Paddy's sister Jean possibly knows him best of all from childhood days to the present time.

They grew up, along with their late sister Linda, in Rathcoole, and both

Paddy and Jean still live in that area, within a few miles of each other. Jean paints amazing pictures with her words about their childhood days. Back then, Rathcoole was just another rural village, and the close proximity of Dublin city made little difference to it.

An unassuming, bright-eyed, kind and witty woman, Jean's stories take the listener back to bygone days in Ireland, when rural life was a lot simpler. She has many stories of her childhood shared with Paddy, an unmined treasure-trove of stories of bygone days in rural County Dublin that could compare with some of those from Cork by author Alice Taylor.

'As children, I suppose we could all sing a bit in our house, and we took that from my mother, who sang a lot. Pat, as we called him then, was well able to sing, but he didn't do so much when were children. Our father had a good voice, but he didn't sing very much either. However, he would hum along while sitting at the table. When an uncle of ours would come home from England, it was like killing the fatted calf, as Dad would sing then and it was quite nice,' says Jean.

Her earliest memory of Paddy is of when he was a very young child and of protecting him from being attacked by a sheep in a field behind their home. 'There was a corn haggard at the back of our house and we would be out there playing with a lot of friends. There was also a ram in the haggard that we were always afraid of. I'd have to spend my time catching Pat by the hand, in case he would be attacked by the ram.

'Pat had a patch over one eye while waiting for some surgery on it, and he couldn't see very well. If he went missing at all, some of the others could see that I would be in a panic. They would say, "Where is Pat Reilly? Jean is looking for him" in case the ram would attack him,' she laughs.

Even though they were considered to be from Dublin, their childhood memories could be from any rural village in Ireland, as Jean explains. 'We had the hay and straw in the haggard beside our house, and used bogies, (sledges or hay floats) to haul the cocks of hay in from the fields. We sat up on them when the horse would be dragging them into the haggard. There would be so many of us on them, and we had great fun when the hay would be knocked down.

'We had great fun too when the threshing mill arrived in the haggard to separate the seed from the stalks of corn and remove the chaff from the seeds. We used to have such fun jumping around in the heaps of chaff and throwing it at each other.

'Pat would hum and sing, and he was a devil-may-care character growing up. But none of the family ever thought that he would become such a successful singer later in life.

'In fact when he was first singing on stage up in Mick McCarthy's place, The Embankment, he never told us. When I first saw his name as Paddy Reilly in the paper as a singer there, I couldn't believe it. Someone else told us first that he was appearing on stage there – he took us all by surprise.'

Jean remembers that their father didn't encourage Paddy to go into a singing career, but their mother didn't seem to mind. 'Our father was very disappointed when Pat left the job in Swiftbrook Paper Mills. He said he should've stayed there in a pensionable job as he didn't really believe that Pat would make a living singing. But even one of the managers there told him he was right to leave. Our mother was a very quiet woman and didn't say much about it, but she did fret quite a bit when he was going to the States, as she thought he might never come back.'

Jean admits that she worried too about his chances of becoming a success as a singer in America. 'I missed him a lot when he went to America. Even though he would write letters home, I was probably thinking, like my mother, about him being so far away, and wondering if he would ever return.

'But of course, he did come back, and both of our parents saw a lot of his earlier success and they were thrilled about it. His wedding to Diane here in Dublin was a big event for us all,' she adds.

Jean remembers Paddy's wedding as an amazing party, attended by so many big stars from the Irish folk and ballad scene. It was held in Saggart, where her family home is, and just 'over the road' from Rathcoole, where they were both born. 'It was brilliant, something I will never forget, and I'm only sorry I don't have photographs or a film of it. There were famous people coming in and out of our house – Luke Kelly, others from The Dubliners and many more – and the event went on 'till six in the morning,' she laughs.

'The wedding ceremony was a great event, and Paddy's beautiful wife, Diane, who sadly passed away since at a young age, looked so pretty. They travelled to the reception in The Embankment on a horse and cart. All the villagers along the route were out waving them on, and the youngsters running after the cart. I can still picture the scene in my mind; it was so lovely.

'Paddy and Diane then went off from Dublin Airport on their honeymoon to Spain, and forgot to take their luggage out of the boot of the car,' says Jean with a laugh.

She adds how delighted they all were to hear that Paddy and Diane were going to make their home in Ireland. 'He was a total home boy, and he had brought his wife Diane, Lord rest her, over here to see if she could adapt to Ireland before they got married. He certainly didn't want to settle permanently in the States, and Diane loved living here also.'

Paddy and Diane riding on a donkey cart on their wedding day.

Even since the days when, as a small child, she was shepherding Paddy away from a dangerous ram in their back garden in Rathcoole, Jean has remained a loyal and devoted sister to him.

'We visit as much as possible. When one of the ladies drives me up here to his house, we sit and have a chat most days. He is shy about all his success, and is a very humble person. Of course, when he is in the pub and has taken a few drinks, he will have the craic, but otherwise I suppose one could say that he remains very private about it all. We are all so proud of him. His success singing "The Fields of Athenry" was just something else. He has a lovely voice, and that is also a beautiful song. It changed his life for ever,' says Jean, with the glint of a sister's pride in her eyes as she hugs her famous younger brother.

It goes without saying that Paddy Reilly has the love and admiration of his family, extended family, fans and friends. But he also has many friends in high places on the international songwriting scene. One of those is an international singer, songwriter, musician, mentor and producer who wrote his first hit. He also wrote hits for Elvis, Cliff Richard, the Bay City Rollers and a Eurovision-winning song, to name but a few of his accolades. That is, of course, songwriter, producer and musician supreme Phil Coulter.

Phil has great memories of writing 'The Town I Loved So Well', which was an iconic song for both Luke Kelly and Paddy as well as becoming Paddy's first hit. 'Paddy and I were reminiscing about "The Town I Loved So Well" when we met some time ago at the K-Club,' says Phil. 'It was a lovely get-together of a few of us in the business. There were about a dozen of us – old pals, old veterans – and how great it was to see Paddy and exchange stories again.'

Phil's song was a chart hit in Ireland not just once for Paddy, but three times! Firstly in April 1974; again in October 1974; and then, almost five years later, he was back in the Irish charts again with the song in August 1979. 'I remember specifically going back to a time when we were talking after a gig in Mick McCarthy's place, The Embankment in Tallaght, and giving him the words of "The Town I Loved So Well". Paddy said to me something like, "You know that great song of yours, 'The Town I Loved So Well', that Luke is singing on The Dubliners album? I'd love to do that."

'We left The Embankment and went to Paddy's house, which was only about ten or twenty minutes from the venue. We sat there, and obviously had a few more jars, and I wrote out the words of "The Town I Loved So Well". Paddy had a guitar and played along as I was teaching him the song. My hand-written lyrics of "The Town I Loved So Well" were handed to him right there, and the song became the start of Paddy's recording successes. When Paddy sings the song, it stays in the mind forever,' says Phil.

'There was another occasion, a long time later, when I wrote another song for Paddy – "Gold and Silver Days", which was particularly tailored for his voice,' he continues. During his later years, the album with 'Gold and Silver Days' as the title track became one of Paddy's biggest-selling albums.

'That song, "Gold and Silver Days", is one that I also do on my own live concerts, in deference to Paddy. It's one of those songs that by the time I get to the second chorus, everybody is joining in.

'It tells its own story that resonates with so many, and it means that it wasn't just a song that was a hit in the charts (for Paddy), but one that has also passed on into the consciousness of the Irish people, that people have a well of affection for. It has become part of the public domain,' says Phil.

'The song was written for Paddy Reilly. It was constructed for him – the whole range, the whole emotion. When I listened to it again not long ago, I said, Jesus Christ, all I can say is that Paddy Reilly had some engine. He shared something with Luke Kelly, which was great enunciation. You never had to ask twice, "What's he saying? What's that word there?" Never.'

Phil Coulter was already no stranger to writing best-selling songs for singing stars, whether ballads, pop, folk, country or rock'n'roll. Back in 1968, long before he did any work with Paddy Reilly, Phil co-wrote 'Congratulations' for Cliff Richard. It was a number-one hit in eight countries, as well as being a runner-up in the Eurovision Song Contest that year.

Other early successes included writing songs for Irish showbands, especially Butch Moore and The Capitol. But international success first came Phil's way with 'Puppet on a String', co-written with Bill Martin, which won the Eurovision Song Contest for England in 1967. It went on to reach number one in the UK pop charts for three weeks. The song has been recorded in over thirty languages, with more than 200 different artists recording it over the years. It went to number one in most European countries, as well as in Argentina and New Zealand. It was also a top-ten hit in countries as far apart as Venezuela, Australia, South Africa and Malaysia.

Paddy's rendition of Phil's song 'The Town I Loved So Well' spent almost five months in the Irish charts. The song has also been recorded by many others worldwide, including versions in French, German, Welsh and Norwegian. It has been recorded by artists in many different music genres, including former three-times Eurovision Song Contest winner Johnny Logan, Dexys Midnight Runners, The Irish Tenors, young Irish folk group The High Kings and young country singing star Nathan Carter.

Almost a decade before Phil gave the handwritten lyrics of 'The Town I Loved So Well' to Paddy Reilly, he and Bill Martin co-wrote the last million-selling song in America for Elvis Presley. 'My Boy' was the biggest hit for Elvis during the final five years of his life. It was a top-twenty hit in the Billboard chart, number five in the UK and number one in the US country charts.

'But as a songwriter, my proudest professional boast, the song that I am personally proudest of, is "The Town I Loved So Well",' says Phil. 'That is above all the other international successes. While I loved Luke's version of the song, it was Paddy that had the big hit with it. Paddy's version was played off the air at a time when RTÉ radio played Irish artists, unlike recent times.'

Phil says that people such as Paddy Reilly wouldn't have a chance of having their songs played on national radio in Ireland if they were starting out today. 'We were on a deputation to the Dáil (Irish House of Parliament) a few years ago – Paddy, Paul Brady, promoter Pat Egan plus a bunch of us were on it. We were making the point that there needs to be legislation to ensure that Irish artists get a fair shot on national stations, which they don't.

'You will hear Irish music tucked away somewhere on the graveyard shift after twelve o'clock at night. There is no support for up-and-coming Irish artists. I made the point in front of this panel of TDs that if Jimmy McCarthy wrote "Ride On" or if Paul Brady wrote "The Island" or Johnny Duhan wrote "The Voyage" or if I wrote "The Town I Loved So Well" today, we wouldn't get those songs f***ing played on radio. Most independent radio stations are far more reflective of what people's tastes are,' says Phil with passion in his voice.

Phil Coulter also produced albums for Paddy Reilly. Among those was one that Paddy remembers well, because they had to relocate the recording session at the last minute from a Dublin studio to one in Belfast.

Phil also remembers that incident, and he still has a laugh about today. 'Oh! the glamour of it all, as we had to rush up to record that album in the middle of a busy industrial estate in Belfast. When we would take our breaks for food during the recording session, we'd go to a nearby Chinese restaurant and when they realised who we were, they were playing our music on the sound system,' he laughs.

'Paddy and I go back a long way, and I have great time for Paddy. His career of course was very much linked to The Dubliners. There were a few off-the-bench players in The Dubliners, with Luke's passing and when Ronnie left, but of all the off-the-bench players that came into the group, Paddy and Jim McCann were the two boys who really carried it off.

'They were the first and second subs on the team and they delivered always.'

Phil's friendship with Paddy has never wavered down through the decades and to the present time. 'Oh yeah, I've always kept in touch with him as much as possible. A few years ago, before the COVID-19 restrictions hit, a number of us, old dogs in the business, would meet for lunch from time to time. On one such occasion, Paddy arrived in a red Porsche. I just looked at him and remarked, "The rare auld times my arse!" It was like something that Paddy would say himself and we all roared with laughter,' says Phil.

He adds that it was great to have lunch with him again more recently, especially after Paddy had another bout of ill health. 'Many of his old buddies were there, all us old dogs, including contemporaries such as promoter Maurice Cassidy, journalist Sam Smyth, comedian Noel V Ginnity and others.

'It was all just a good laugh and it was so great to see Paddy in good form, laughing and enjoying the craic. As Paddy Boland the doctor said, "This will have done Paddy more good than every bit of surgery, or more than any hospital or doctor could do." I'm so glad we could all get together and give him a good lift and hopefully we will have many more such moments.'

Paddy's son Ciarán and daughter Ashling are extremely close to their famous father. But in Ashling's case, it is a closeness from far across the ocean, as she lives and works in the USA. When the COVID-19 restrictions on travel were in place, it jettisoned any chances of the two meeting up for almost two years. So it was unbridled joy when Ashling and her husband and their son finally got back home to Rathcoole for a visit in November 2021.

It was a proud moment for Paddy too, as he was able to see her in her cap and gown and with her scroll, as she had just graduated with a Master's degree from the prestigious Harvard University in the USA.

Through phone calls and messages, Ashling managed as well as possible to stay connected with her dad and brother during the long lockdown, and especially while Paddy was in hospital for a number of months.

'Ashling dressed up with her cap and gown, just as she would have done on graduation day, but here at Dad's house, and had some photos taken with him, which was great,' says Ciarán.

Ciarán, who lives not far from his father's house in Rathcoole, is more than just a son to his dad. He is a confidant, a companion, a carer and a business advisor. The Reillys, father and son, are just good buddies and have been over the years.

When they were growing up, Ciarán says that he and Ashling never took much notice of having a famous father. 'The village we grew up in was one where we were related to lots of other people. We knew almost everyone and everybody was famous in their own way.

'When I was a kid, The Embankment, where Dad was playing, was just up the road and was a big focal point in the area. Saggart and Rathcoole were just small villages back then, and it was very normal for Dad to be working locally as a singer in The Embankment,' says Ciarán.

Ciarán's first memories of The Embankment were of going there as child of eight or nine years of age to see his dad on stage. 'It was in the days long before the smoking ban in pubs. You would be hit by big clouds of smoke when you went in there, as was typical of venues then. But there was always a great atmosphere and an electric energy in the place. It was always a lively and friendly place to go to, even if the first hole in the ozone layer may well have been in the sky over The Embankment!' he laughs.

The master of ceremonies was Mick McCarthy, who he vividly remembers as a larger-than-life, charismatic character, who welcomed everybody with open arms.

'I remember him being so welcoming to everyone. He would be chatting with people with a glass of whiskey in one hand and a cigarette in the other. He would be showing people to their seats and just making them feel comfortable there.

'Dad was headlining at The Embankment at that time, and you would have people like The Dubliners coming in, as well as other acts. We would see Dad playing and the reaction that he would get made us realise that what he was doing, he was doing very well and he was getting a lot of attention for it.

'It was all very normal to us, as it was happening in the village where we were growing up. It was only about two miles from our house, close to the school that I walked to every morning. It was just what was happening in our world as kids – just life in our little world of a few square miles around us,' says Ciarán.

He remembers many times when his dad's famous pals from the music scene would come to their home to visit. One such memory sticks out in his mind – the time he sneaked up out of bed as a kid one night in 1980 to watch a big boxing match from across the Atlantic on the TV.

'It was a late-night satellite broadcast of a boxing match between Sugar Ray Leonard and Roberto Duran. Dad was watching it in our home with Luke Kelly, Jim McCann, Patsy Watchorn and others. These lads were arriving with a half a dozen bottles of Guinness under their arms, and they came to watch the fight at about two or three in the morning when it was televised. I sneaked up behind the couch and watched the fight with them too, but they never knew I was there. They were just shouting at the TV and having a few drinks and took no notice of me,' laughs Ciarán.

Ciarán also has fond memories of summer holidays spent in America with his sister and their mum and watching Paddy performing over there. 'Dad would be doing weeks of residencies in Cape Cod and in particular at the Century Club there, which was great as it was a venue similar to The Embankment back home. As my mother is from Boston, we would spent two or three weeks of the summer holidays in the USA. We would spend some of the time with Dad where he would be performing and the rest of the time visiting with our American relations. We would do that probably every second year and it was lovely, especially seeing so much nice weather and going to the beach. As kids, we would be getting a hamburger and a milkshake. We were experiencing for real what we had seen people do on American TV shows that were screened back home in Ireland.'

Ciarán says that, despite his touring abroad, their dad was still around most of the time in Ireland, when they wanted him to kick a ball around with them in the back garden or take them to football matches.

'He was always around when gigging in Ireland and even when going back and forth to England. His big trip would be to America after Christmas, and he might go for two months or more. That's where he had to go to make much of his year's earnings. But he was lucky not to have to emigrate permanently to work, as he could do a few months up to St Patrick's Day in America. Then he would be back here for most of the rest of the year, except he would do the summer residencies in Cape Cod. But he would be round at home for most of the football matches that we would be going to.

'Dad would have me in Croke Park on many Sundays and would be lifting me over the turnstile, just like my grandfather did with him when he was a child.'

After 1984, life did get a bit more hectic for Paddy, as Ciarán explains: 'That was when things really took off for Dad with "The Fields of Athenry". From watching him playing locally and at the residencies in America, we then saw him playing much bigger venues everywhere.

'I remember going to see him in the Olympia Theatre, which I think was in 1984 when he did a week of concerts there. I was only a kid, bit I can still remember things really kicking off for him with "The Fields of Athenry". We were all so proud and glad for him. Isn't it great to get a song like that, which meant so much for Dad's career? Those were very happy days.'

He was also present with his dad, but this time in America, when Paddy had another massive hit with the emigration song 'Flight of the Earls', and Ciarán has a funny memory about that.

'We answered a phone call in our hotel from Dad's manager Jim Hand one day while Dad was playing in the States. It was the time that the song was a hit back in Ireland. Jim's advice to Dad on the phone, which we were also listening in to, was about what he needed to do with his image. Now that Dad was topping the charts again, Jim's advice to him was typical and it was just hilarious.

'He said to Dad, "It's time to dip the fleece again, Pat." While that may not make sense to others, it did to us, because as a family we knew instantly what Jim meant. He had the same advice when "The Fields" was a hit. Jim meant that Dad needed to dye his white hair and make it black again!'

Ciarán was well used to seeing Jim Hand around their home when he was a kid, and hearing some of his hilarious expressions. In those early years, he also inherited his love of horse racing from his dad. Ciarán was a winner right from the start!

'I cleared about fifty pence, as I had one pound on the winner and got one pound fifty back at the first race that Dad took me to. Shergar was running and was the favourite, and he won the Derby at ridiculously low odds. My dad had me on his shoulders that day. I can remember him roaring at the jockey, Lester Piggott, saying something like, "Go, Lester, go, go!"

'It was a big deal when he won, because Shergar was a big celebrity in our area – he was kept over in Ballymany Stud in The Curragh. He won the race by half the track,' says Ciarán, as Paddy interjects, 'Correct, and no horse ever won that race since by as much.'

Ciarán and his dad go racing together regularly ever since. 'We would go to Cheltenham for two days most years, usually Thursday and Friday. We go to so many race meeting together and always enjoy those trips,' he says.

Apart from all the leisure time spent with his father, Ciarán is now also involved in the admin side of his dad's music. 'I help him with publishing and in the music side of the business. I am involved in dealing with the record company and all that. We get on well together, never have had any falling out as far as I can remember, except the odd minor row over horses maybe.

'We were always a very close family and even though Ashling is living in America, we remain in touch all the time. We had great times growing up together and still have all those great memories and remain very close,' says Ciarán.

He adds that they are both very proud of their father's success as a recording artist and as a touring performer, as well as of the many awards he has been presented with during his career.

'Dad got a Lifetime Achievement Award from IBAM, the Irish Books, Arts & Music Society in Chicago, for his contribution to Irish music back in 2014, which was very special. He has won lots of awards here at home also.

'I think he has done great things for Irish music both at home and abroad, as his interpretations of songs are very different to a lot of other people. Many of his fans say so, especially in America, where Dad made a career for himself as well.

'They like his interpretation of the great Irish ballads, many of which have been hits again over the past forty or fifty years, along with the newer ones of course. We as a family are just very proud of his contribution to the Irish music scene in general,' concludes Ciarán.

'Sure I had to do something to help feed ye lot!' replies Paddy with his hallmark loud guffaw of a laugh.

Another man who has been a companion, close friend, a studio musician on many recordings and a touring partner with Paddy in The Dubliners is John Sheahan. John, famous for 'The Marino Waltz' and many other tunes, was the last of the long-standing members of The Dubliners when the group's name was retired in 2012. But John didn't retire – he has pursued diverse musical and poetic projects since then. He also has some great tales to tell about working with Paddy from over nine years in The Dubliners and various studio sessions over many decades.

'We had known Paddy as a singer since the 1960s, when we were doing a regular Monday night gig in The Embankment in Tallaght. He would often get up on stage and sing a song or two with us.

'That was the first time I heard him singing. Straight away, it struck us that this was not an ordinary guy in a pub getting up to sing a song with the band. This fellow had a special voice. It's a gift that some performers, both singers and instrumentalists, have – a distinctive voice or sound, and when you hear them on the radio or on stage they are instantly recognisable. Other singers have nice voices, but they lack that distinctive element where you can identify them straight away,' says John.

He added that there is a very rich baritone-tenor timbre in Paddy's voice.

'I played on a lot of Paddy's recordings, and of course Eamonn Campbell produced many of his albums going back over the years. Eamonn often employed me for those sessions, long before he also became a member of The Dubliners.

'Paddy always picked great songs. There was one that I always loved to hear him sing – "Autumn Has Come", written by Shay Healy. It's a beautiful song.'

John laughs at the suggestion that Paddy might have been asked if he was going to grow a beard when he joined The Dubliners. 'Somebody may have remarked to Paddy that he might be the odd man out without a beard. I can only imagine the colourful reaction they got from Paddy! None of us would have said he had to grow a beard or that it would be a condition of joining The Dubliners.

'Going back over the years, there were several occasions, long before there was any talk of Paddy joining the group, if Luke or Ronnie were off sick, our first call would be to Paddy. He would happily come along and we would take to the stage with very little rehearsals or arrangements beforehand. He would busk his way through the gig without any bother. We would just say, what key is this one in Paddy? That was how causal our approach was, as we all knew each other so well.'

While Paddy often remarks that he was never a great guitar player, John says The Dubliners were always happy with his guitar playing. 'He would semi-apologise at times, saying he wasn't a great guitarist, but there was no need for him to ever say so, as what he did on guitar was adequate for the wonderful voice that he had. There was never any need for that voice to be pushed in any way by amazing guitar playing either. His twin musical talents fitted in very well together.'

John says that when Paddy joined The Dubliners, it was a great asset for the group in general, because his hits and his style of singing became an extra feature of their shows. 'With this new singer Paddy Reilly joining us, he brought with him his own repertoire of hit songs as well. There was a whole new freshness to the shows and to the group.

'There is something else that happened with nearly everyone who joined the group over the years – we all became part of the extended family of The Dubliners. Going back to the very early days with Ronnie and Luke and Ciaran and Barney, whenever there was a celebration, be it a christening or a marriage, within the greater family of The Dubliners, everyone was there celebrating together. It was one of those unique relationships, and Paddy was very much part of that, right from the early days.'

The songs that Paddy brought to The Dubliners included massive hits such as 'The Town I Loved So Well', 'Flight of the Earls' and, of course, 'The Fields of Athenry'. Those songs went down a treat on their European tours, according to John.

'Our main touring areas would have been Germany, Austria, Holland and Scandinavia. He was amazed when he started touring with us at the reaction and the crowds we attracted, anything from 1,000- up to 3,000- or 4,000-seater venues, booked out weeks before we would get there in some cases.'

Paddy had told the others about how, after 'The Fields of Athenry' became a massive hit, his manager Jim Hand had no qualms about raising his appearance fee significantly. Jim quoted a substantially increased fee to promoter Pat Jennings in Castlebar for booking Paddy, and Pat replied that 'those must be the dearest f***ing fields in Ireland'.

'Paddy had a great sense of humour,' says John. 'Sometimes when he was about to sing "The Fields" with us in The Dubliners, when it might not have been on the set list, I would quietly ask him what was he going to sing next. Paddy would whisper, "the dearest". We would all smile, as we knew he meant "The Fields of Athenry". I'm sure the audiences didn't know what we were laughing about among ourselves on stage.'

There is a tune called 'Sporting Paddy' on The Dubliners' *Alive-Alive-O* album, but John Sheahan says that neither Barney McKenna or himself had any interest in watching sports when on tour. Paddy and the others had, however.

'I had no interest in football at all. They would all be speaking another language, which would be going over my head. It was the same if they were talking about tennis or rugby or any sport.

'But just for the craic while we were on the road, I would quietly be asking our coach driver and sound engineer Tom O'Brien to give me a few sports names, as he was an expert in all those things. He would give me a few names and I would drop those into the conversations with the others as if I was knowledgeable on the subject. They would all be looking around and saying, "Where the f*** did you hear that?"

'Barney was similar to me regarding his knowledge of sport. I remember being in Holland when the World Cup was on, and a whole afternoon was taken over by watching this football match. Barney whispered to me, "What's a striker?" I replied that while I wasn't sure, I thought it was the guy who specialised in scoring goals. Anyway, while we were watching the big game on TV that afternoon, this player scores an amazing goal. Barney shouts out in a very knowledgeable voice, "Jesus, yer man is some striker!" They were all looking around and saying, "Where the f*** did he pick up those sports sayings?" and we smiled quietly.

'There was always craic like that going on when we were on tour,' laughs John, who retains a long-standing friendship with both Paddy and his son Ciarán.

'Paddy and I go back a long way, and his two children, Ciarán and Ashling, are two great young people also. The fun memories that we have of touring with Paddy are just brilliant. The stories about Jim Hand telling him to "dip the fleece", or the one about "The Fields of Athenry" being the "dearest f***ing fields in Ireland", are priceless. Those bring a smile to my face every time I recall them.'

Chapter 10

Irish Sports Stars Sing Paddy's Praises

As a teenager in Dublin and in London, soccer star Niall Quinn says he and his pals would sing along with Paddy's Reilly's 'The Fiends of Athenry', even at nightclubs.

The year 1983 was a momentous one for both Paddy and Niall. It was the year that Paddy's iconic version of the 'The Fields of Athenry' started its seventy-two-week sojourn in the Irish charts. That same year, sixteen-year-old Niall Quinn played in the All-Ireland Minor hurling final with his native Dublin against Galway.

Dublin lost, but a month later Niall was signed as a professional footballer in the UK. He had earlier declined a contract to play Australian rules football.

'Four weeks after the All-Ireland hurling final, I was playing under-eighteen soccer with Arsenal and living in London with my auntie and uncle, who were big rugby supporters. We lived close to the pitch at Twickenham, and my uncle actually worked in the bar at London-Irish at one stage.

'I came home from England that first Christmas and all my friends were singing "The Fields of Athenry". A group of us would go out for a drink to the Spawell Hotel (in Dublin) and, oh Jesus, everybody was singing it – even in the nightclubs. It really made its mark,' says Niall.

The first time Niall heard it sung by a crowd at a major sports event was at an international rugby game in Twickenham during his early years in London. Niall remembers the song becoming 'an anthem in the terraces and stands' at rugby and soccer matches involving Ireland.

Back in London, Niall says he would go out with friends sometimes to the Irish clubs and ballrooms. In one of London's best-known Irish venues of the '80s, the National Ballroom in Kilburn – where acts as diverse as Johnny Cash, The Pogues, Big Tom, David Bowie and Kurt Cobain played – Niall first saw Paddy Reilly perform live.

'I saw him there and in many other venues around London during my early years in England, in '83, '84 and '85.'

During this time, Niall also made his way on to the Irish senior soccer side, with Jack Charlton giving him his first game with Ireland in 1986. A friendship with Paddy Reilly, who was singing one of his favourite songs, soon followed.

'To my great delight when I broke into the Irish soccer team, I was rubbing shoulders with players such as Liam Brady, who would say after a match to come to the Lansdowne Hotel in Dublin where Paddy was playing. Those lovely nights out after matches, when Paddy held court there, are brilliant memories. Sometimes I might not get out of there till daybreak the next day, and Paddy wouldn't either,' laughs Niall.

'You could say that I was second-hand introduced to him by Liam Brady. But when Liam left the squad, some of us younger guys got ideas about ourselves trying to be cool. I didn't see Paddy as much for a while when we started going to nightclubs like Lillie's Bordello.'

Niall's success with Arsenal, Manchester City and Sunderland football clubs lasted for over seventeen years. Niall recalls how Paddy Reilly's hit continued to grow in popularity with Irish fans everywhere during those years. 'It became synonymous with travelling Irish soccer fans everywhere during the Jack Charlton era. They sang it all over Europe and around the world.

'The strength of the song is that it has remained as an anthem at big world sporting events that Irish teams are involved in ever since. Celtic supporters in Scotland also sing it and Liverpool fans have their version of it.'

In earlier times, Paddy was already a firm favourite with Irish soccer players and managers. 'Paddy had other songs that were popular during Eoin Hand's and John Giles's times,' says Niall. 'But when he had the hit with "The Fields of Athenry", that became the definitive version of the song. Nobody can sing it like Paddy,' he added.

Niall recalls an incident late one night in England, when Irish and English were socialising and the atmosphere started to turn sour. Into the breach steps Paddy with a demonstration of the power of music.

'When Paddy sings, people tend to hush and listen; his command of an audience is incredible. I was in Cheltenham with him many years ago, very late one night, and we were in a raucous sing-song at the bar when some English clientele got a little bit of the huffs with all the Irish songs.

'The situation could have gone either way. But Paddy sang them a song, and suddenly you could hear a pin drop among a pub full of raucous people with drink on them. Everything stopped; nobody moved or said a word as Paddy sang "Sweet Thames Flow Softly". His rendition of that song just melted them. He turned what could have become a dangerous situation into another glorious evening that everyone enjoyed.

'When asked what my favourite Cheltenham moment is, I always opt for that. It's great to look back over the races and the winners, and Istabraq's success was great, and so was that of Dawn Run. But in terms of my most memorable moment from those famous racing festivals, it's always lovely to look back on how Paddy calmed the crowd with that beautiful song. Nobody could sing it like him.'

In 1999, Niall scored twenty-one goals in a record-breaking season for his club, Sunderland. He won two major sportswriters awards for his playing that year.

His goal for Ireland in the 1990 FIFA World Cup against The Netherlands got his country through to the second round of that tournament. Fast forward to 2002, in the autumn of his international career at age thirty-five, and he scored against Cyprus to become, at that time, Ireland's all-time top goal scorer.

After retirement from the soccer scene, in 2008, Niall went on to win a County Kildare Junior C Gaelic Football medal with his club Eadestown. 'Yeah, I came back after retirement and did that. Paddy gave me a bit of ribbing about it – all good humouredly. He knows so much about the GAA, and indeed about many other sports as well.'

Both sides of Niall's parent's families provided county hurlers for Tipperary, with his father playing in an All-Ireland final. 'My father won two minor All-Irelands and got into the Tipperary senior team and scored three goals in a National League final at eighteen years of age. We still have the cutting from the *Irish Independent* of 5 May 1954, when he scored those three goals. But a year later they lost the Munster final to Cork, with a goal in extra time by the great Christy Ring. My dad hopped on a boat to England shortly afterwards to get work, and he wasn't twenty years old at the time,' says Niall.

He came back to Dublin a few years later, but couldn't revive his hurling career due to restrictions regarding playing for Tipperary while living in Dublin.

'Just when he started playing with Dublin, a new rule was brought in that you couldn't play with them unless you were from Dublin. So my dad's county hurling career didn't restart, even though he was very promising in the early stages,' says Niall.

Niall's own soccer career reached dizzy heights of success in England, and his autobiography also won the top award in its category at the inaugural British Sports Books Awards.

Niall is also known for his charitable work in raising funds for worthy causes, especially for sick children, and he has won many awards, including an honorary MBE.

Niall's success with the Irish soccer team and with top UK clubs Arsenal, Manchester City and particularly Sunderland is legendary. A few hours after being interviewed for this book, Niall was one of four iconic Irish soccer stars from the Jack Charlton era being presented with special medals in honour of all the joy they brought to the nation. The others were Packie Bonner, David O'Leary and Shay Given. So self-effacing is Niall that he never mentioned during this book's interview that he would be getting the award from President Higgins on TV that night.

Like Paddy Reilly, he is modest, almost bashful in fact, when his achievements are mentioned to him. But he is happy to speak of his affection for Paddy Reilly and his admiration for Paddy's talent as a singer. Niall was always impressed by how humble and grounded Paddy always remained amid 'all the fame that he has had for his singing'.

'I've met him often at golf outings, as well as at social occasions with others, from both the entertainment and sports scenes. These events were a natural coming together of all of us, who others might say didn't have real jobs,' he laughs. 'People in the entertainment scene, like Paddy, Finbar Furey and Kathy Durkin, are among those I would meet on such occasions. There was almost a squad of people from the entertainment industry that would come together with us sporting guys, and those were always memorable events.

'I've always had good craic with Paddy when we would meet. He has always had that twinkle in his eye, and he is a lovely man to meet socially, considering all the fame that he has had in life with his singing.

'To do all that Paddy has done, yet still remain so grounded and socially amenable to everyone, is one of his great attributes. He gave the world the definitive version of "The Fields of Athenry", and made it a sporting anthem.' That's praise indeed from the great Niall Quinn.

* * *

When it comes to the greatest Dublin footballers and team managers of all time, Tony Hanahoe must be high on everybody's list. But the unassuming lawyer, All-Ireland-winning player and manager is reluctant to discuss any such suggestion. However, when it comes to talking about favourite singers and favourite people, Tony is proud to say that fellow Dub Paddy Reilly is up there in his top list.

'I can't say enough good things about Paddy. He was, and still is, the quintessential approachable gentleman, who had so much fame in the music field. Yet he has always worn that crown well, and never lost his humanity, humility or dignity,' says Tony.

Their friendship goes back to long before Tony's success on the playing fields and as a football manager in the 1970s, but Tony says he never ventured to join in with Paddy singing after any of the Dubs' victories. 'In fairness, as far as I was concerned, Paddy had the singing all to himself – I'd never be a challenger to Paddy's prowess in that area,' he laughs. 'Some of my teammates – Jimmy Keaveney and his friends – might have joined in with him singing when they would meet at the Listowel Races.

'Paddy had a special gift of being a real Dub. But coming from Rathcoole in the county, he had the agricultural side to him as well. You could say that he was well-briefed from both sides of the fence. He had that capability of entertaining people from different backgrounds and appealing to them all.'

Tony recalls that he sometimes met Paddy during trips abroad. 'I met him a few times in America, as we had a number of mutual friends who worked and lived there. Paddy's lengthy career took off in so many countries that you'd never know where you would bump into him.'

Tony's own lengthy career as a top-flight footballer reached one of its many highs in 1974, when he won his first All-Ireland senior medal with Dublin. Afterwards he won two All-Ireland medals back to back in 1976 and '77, and he had the distinction of also being the player-manager of the team during the latter year.

'To tell you the truth now, I wonder how I did that, or if it was a wise move to be player, manager, captain, selector – the whole lot. We achieved what we set out to achieve anyway, but looking back on it now, as I was also a professional lawyer at the same time, I don't know where I found enough time to put in all the work,' says Tony.

He says that he and his teammates got tremendous support from the Dublin County Board during those years. Up to 1974, it had been over a decade of bare times for Dublin football regarding winning All-Irelands.

In that breakthrough year, Tony Hanahoe was a vital cog in the team, and in the win against Galway, even though he is reluctant to say so. But his Galway opponent, double All-Star player from the early 1970s Tommy Joe Gilmore, is not at all reticent when talking about how Hanahoe outfoxed him on the field and helping Dublin achieve that victory.

Tommy Joe was the high-fielding centre-half-back on the Galway team, a fulcrum around which the defence should have rotated that day if the ball was sent in high to the Dublin forwards. But instead, the Dubs targeted more low ball into each side of the Galway defence and the centre-half-back was taken 'all over the place' by his marker Tony Hanahoe.

'He didn't stay still for a moment, moving almost all over the field and taking me out of defence in the process. It worked, even though in doing so, Tony had to play a negative role regarding his own scoring. But he was the sort of selfless player that would sacrifice that aspect of his game if it was for the good of the team, and on that day it was,' laughs Tommy Joe, who often talked about those tactics with Tony since, especially when they meet at golf outings.

Tony and his teammates were delighted to see the success Paddy had with a song about fields far from Dublin with in the '80s. 'I was listening to

Paddy singing long before he had that hit, and of course his version is my favourite. But Paddy has also been a spectacular success with so many other songs, both as a solo singer and as a member of The Dubliners.

'He has always been very laid-back in his live performances. I can only describe him as a natural type of singer, who never needed to be pretentious in any way to put across a song perfectly. He never allowed fame or fortune to turn his head either,' concludes Tony.

* * *

Like many of the world's most successful people, top racehorse trainer Willie Mullins, a friend and business associate of Paddy, is shy when talking about his own sensational success. He is reticent almost to the point of embarrassment when his own international achievements are mentioned. But he opens up, with wit and good humour, about how proud he is of the successes of his long-time friend Paddy.

With his total wins at Cheltenham now at eighty-eight, Willie is the most successful trainer ever at the top UK festival of racing. Indeed, Willie's total of ten winners at the 2022 event was as many for him alone as all of the UK trainers got between them.

But when all of this is mentioned to Willie, he quickly moves on to talk instead about his joy when some of their friends got Paddy to sing one night in the hotel after the races.

'We had him going this year in Cheltenham. He was in great form at a party among us one night and we got him to sing "The Fields of Athenry" and other songs. There were one or two other fellows who tried to join in, but we had to have a Steward's Enquiry and suspend them for a song or two! Their fine was that they had to buy the next few rounds at the bar,' laughs Willie.

This scene is corroborated by a story by David Walsh in the *Sunday Times*. Walsh's story says that besides 'the festival's leading trainer' Willie Mullins and his wife Jackie, Michael Carrick, the former Manchester United and England midfielder, was also at the same hotel, as he and his brother Greame had taken their dad Vince to the festival for his seventieth birthday. After dinner on Thursday, the Mullinses, the Reillys, the Carricks and friends assembled in the hotel bar. One drink followed another, but the highlight of the night was Paddy singing 'The Fields of Athenry' for Vince Carrick's birthday.

Reilly is now at a point in his life where he doesn't just break into song because some punter asks. But on this occasion, Reilly sang the song and stilled the bar. Willie Mullins stayed 'till the death'. He thinks it was about 2.30am when he turned in, but 'who could be sure at that hour?'

Willie of course currently trains horses for Paddy, and his son Ciaran. So far, the most successful of those is Stones and Roses, which has already won at meetings in Cork and Punchestown, and Willie has high hopes for. 'He is the sort of a horse that if he gets into the Irish Grand National, he could win it. But it's a very hard race to get into, let alone win,' he says. He adds that Paddy has always enjoyed his wins with horses and knows how to celebrate them, which is an important quality in an owner.

'You've got to live life when wins happen, and Paddy is always well able to do that. Now that they have horses in training with me, I meet Paddy and his son Ciaran more often at the races, and afterwards when the horses run. We have had a few celebratory drinks after wins, and even after we didn't win,' he laughs.

Willie reflects on the long association that his late father Paddy Mullins had with the Reilly family. Paddy Mullins Snr sold the horse 'Louis Fourteen' to Paddy Reilly and trained him to win the Beginners' Chase at Listowel back in 1999. 'It was through Paddy's interest in the horses my father trained for him that our paths crossed first,' says Willie.

'My father trained horses all my life and I suppose you could use the old expression that I was born on the back of a horse! I was an amateur jockey in my younger years. But then as you get older, your values change, just like many footballers, and you go into training. I've gotten so much pleasure since I started training; I enjoy it much more than when I was going over fences at forty miles an hour on a horse.'

His wife Jackie was also a champion jockey, and they are also quietly proud of the success of their son Patrick, the winning jockey in the Hunters' Chase in Cheltenham in 2022.

'Patrick is a trainer as well as an amateur jockey, and he loves that. For such a tall fellow, he is very committed, because at six-foot-one plus, he's had to be very committed to keep his weight down.

'He also writes articles for the newspapers from a jockey's perspective, like when he won the Galway Hurdle or when he was a jockey at Aintree. Those articles, written from the horse's back, so to speak, almost bring you into the saddle when reading them,' he says.

Willie says that he got to know Paddy better following his international success with 'The Fields of Athenry'. 'It was obvious when a singer as good as Paddy did such a fine job on "The Fields of Athenry" that he was going to have success abroad with it, especially in places such as America and Australia. You just can't keep a good man down, and it is no surprise that he has enjoyed such phenomenal success abroad in many countries, as well as at home.'

Willie says it was a joy to meet Paddy in Cheltenham again for the 2022 festival. 'Due to the lockdown, people like Paddy and my own mother were not getting out or having interaction with people, and it impacts on them. My mother, Maureen, would be in the same age bracket and she loves to get out, as does Paddy.

'Since the restrictions were lifted, it's like switching on a light for my mother or for Paddy, to be able to get out to race meetings again,' says Willie.

One of the first race meetings he brought her to after the restrictions were lifted was an early meeting in Punchestown this year, and Ciaran had also brought Paddy to it.

'After the race, Paddy was there on his walking sticks, and it was my mother's first day out too. Paddy said, "Come on, Maureen, and we'll go for a drink." I said, I can go with ye, and she said, "No, we are all right," and so I left them at the owners' and trainers' bar. When I came back an hour and a half later, they were still there, nattering away. It was fantastic to see them both there, racing, chatting and simply delighted to be getting out again,' says Willie.

Asked if he was tempted to break into a few lines of 'The Fields of Athenry', in order to encourage Paddy to sing it on that occasion, he replies, 'I wouldn't even dare to try to sing any of Paddy's hit songs. I'll leave that to the master.'

Chapter 11

Retirement, Racing, Reminiscing and Beating Cancer

P addy's love of racing and reading has continued during retirement. As a racehorse owner, he has won at some major race meetings – once without even being at the race!

A voracious reader, he is often stuck in a book until two or three in the morning. As his son Ciarán remarks with a laugh, 'Dad still keeps musician's hours regarding getting up and going to bed.'

Sitting in his comfortable home in Rathcoole, surrounded by books on diverse topics, Paddy opens up about the biggest battle he has fought in life

– getting cancer and beating it. But as he reminisces about his earlier battles to survive as a ballad singer, before his big break came with 'The Fields', it's obvious that Paddy's love of racing always had a therapeutic impact on all his big battles in life. He currently owns two racehorses, and has been involved with winners and losers since he was a youngster.

'Living here in Rathcoole all our life, almost everybody had a share in a horse. We might own the tail or the left leg of a horse. Neighbours, friends – everybody had a leg of a horse. There might be twenty people involved,' he laughs.

When asked if any of them won much money from being members of those horse-owning syndicates, Paddy laughs. 'Money, what's that? I've said it often, and I'll say it again – horses would break the Bank of England, and anyone who thinks otherwise is not thinking clearly. Horses can be a nightmare, but sometimes there is light at the end of the tunnel too, even if you are facing the light from an oncoming train!'

Paddy might have seen, and perhaps was part-owner of, some losers, but some of his horses were winners too. These include Louis Fourteen and Athenry Boy, the latter named in honour of his big hit. Another, Stones and Roses, co-owned with his son Ciarán is a current winner, as reported by irishracing.com in November 2019. The report states that 'Paddy Reilly's Dublin colours were carried to success at Cork as the famous balladeer renewed old acquaintances with Willie Mullins and his family.'

This was a winning partnership, as their horse Stones And Roses won the Irish Stallion Farms EBF Beginners Chase.

Stones and Roses has showed real promise, winning at race meetings in Punchestown and Cork, with jockey Brian Hayes on board on both occasions. 'Ciarán and I are happy that we bought Stones and Roses,' says Paddy. 'We also have a second horse with Willie Mullins, but she hasn't raced yet; she is just eating her oats and doing some light exercise. But we might race her later this year. The general idea is to get them into some of the race meetings around Ireland and to enjoy it. You will never make a fortune out of it, that's for sure.'

Paddy was also winning at the popular Listowel Races back in 1999, with his horse Louis Fourteen, winning the Beginners' Chase.

Paddy laughs when he recalls that the win took him by surprise – up until the finish, his horse didn't look as if it was going to win. 'There was a horse that must have been about twenty lengths ahead of the field, but then, at the second-last fence, he fell. The one that was chasing him fell at the last fence, and that left our lad to go on and win the race. I was there at the race, but hadn't backed my horse. Since I was about fifteen years old, I had been going to the Listowel Races, and I would know many people there. So it was a great thrill to have won in Listowel with Louis Fourteen.'

While Paddy can't remember the exact year when he bought his first horse, it was long before Ciarán was born. Paddy Mullins trained his horses for many years. 'I enjoyed being in the company of Mr Mullins, as he was an absolute gentleman. Now we have horses with his son Willie. The Mullinses are a great family to work with and great friends also.

'I had a winner at the Galway Races in 2017 with Athenry Boy, which was very appropriate, but I wasn't even there to see him win,' says Paddy.

He was obviously very happy that his horse had won at the Galway Races during a Saturday meeting, but at that moment he was far away in Croke Park, watching his beloved Dublin footballers playing.

'I was in Galway for the week of the races and we were hoping that Athenry Boy would get to race all week, but it didn't happen. While he seemed to be in line to do so on Saturday, we feared he was going to get "balloted out" yet again. He was already balloted out twice at Galway earlier in the week and so I went back to Dublin that morning, as I thought he would be balloted out a third time.' (Being 'balloted out' can happen if there are too many entries for a race which might, for example, be set at a maximum of twenty horses. The officials decide, based on past performances, which horses are allowed to enter, with higher-ranking horses staying and weaker ones being balloted out.)

That day, in the stand at Croke Park, Paddy heard from another spectator that his horse was the winner at the race meeting that he had left only a few hours earlier. 'A friend of mine shouted across, "Jez, your horse is after winning in Galway at twenty to one!" and my reaction was, "You are f***ing joking." I didn't have a penny of a bet on him as we thought he was going to be balloted out. He won and it was really funny when I rang a friend of mine, John Breslin, who was home from America and was at the Galway Races.

'John replied, "F*** you anyway. Not alone did your horse win, but my horse was the five-to-four favourite for that race. I had a big bet on him, but he was beaten into third place and your f***ing horse won." Talk about me rubbing salt into the wounds, innocently ringing him up to find out what horse had won the race,' laughs Paddy.

Meanwhile, Dublin were beating Monaghan by a cricket score at Croke Park. 'The match was a bit of a fiasco, as Dublin were ten points ahead at half-time. When they came out for the second half, they just started kicking the ball diagonally across their own half of the field. I decided that I wasn't going to wait for the second thirty-five minutes of this slaughter, and I left. But the damage was done to my afternoon – my horse had won in Galway and I was back home in Dublin!'

Paddy also had a horse that finished second at 'Glorious' Goodwood, one of England's top race tracks. He might have won that day, but a catalogue of events resulted in a change of jockey at that last moment.

'The horse was Spacious Sky, and it was trained by Tony Martin. I wanted Kieren Fallon to ride him, but on his way to the race meeting, he got stuck in traffic and failed to arrive on time. Kieran is a good friend of mine, and he was the best jockey in England. I really wanted him in the saddle that day, but it was just unfortunate that the traffic caused a last minute change of jockey for the race.

'We were in the parade ring with the horse when an announcement went out over the loudspeakers: "Will trainer Tony Martin please come to the weighing room," and I knew something was wrong. My first thought was that maybe somebody had forgotten the horse's passport. But Tony came back into the ring and said that we had to get another jockey – and fast.

'He got Richard Hughes, who was also a champion jockey at the time. He gave the horse a great ride, but unfortunately he put him six or seven pounds overweight. The horse was second, only beaten by two lengths. But if Kieren had been on him, there wouldn't have been that extra weight and he would have won,' says Paddy.

'That's just one of many hard-luck stories in horse racing. It's one of many that got away – sometimes I think they all got away,' he adds with a laugh.

In the USA, Paddy says that he had 'a lovely horse' that also finished second in a regular race at the Gulf Stream track in Miami, Florida. He was ridden by one of America's most famous jockeys, who also has links to Ireland via his wife who is from a racing family who are friends of Paddy.

Johnny Velazquez was the top-earning jockey in the USA in 2004 and 2005, and is still in the top ten there. In 2020 and 2021, he had another notable double, winning the Kentucky Derby both years. Paddy takes up the story:

'Johnny is married to Leona O'Brien, the daughter of a fellow that I went to school with, trainer Leo O'Brien. He is a top trainer in America, and still trains at Belmont. Leo sent a horse over here too, named Four Star All Star, and it won the 2000 Guineas race. The same horse won five or six years on the trot in Saratoga. They even have a street in Saratoga named Four Star All Star,' he says.

So, in retirement, racing is still a major interest for Paddy, and he loves to talk about it. He is hopeful of more success this year, perhaps with the two horses that he and Ciarán currently have with trainer Willie Mullins. Paddy might have a flutter on his own horses, but only occasionally. 'I wouldn't let my heart rule my head if my own horses were running,' he says.

Paddy says that over the years he would usually have 'two or three horses' at the same time, sometimes as part of a syndicate. He admits that it can be a costly hobby, but he adds with a glint in his eye that 'There's no point in being a fool unless you can prove it!'

Another great pastime for Paddy, especially now during his retirement, is reading, and many books about horse racing are included in his collection. Pointing toward the biography of Tony McCoy on the bookshelf in his sitting room, Paddy says, 'I would have read the biographies of most of the famous jockeys, such as McCoy. I'm happy to say also that many of them were great friends of mine, including McCoy and Kieren Fallon.

'Racing is a tough game and It's great to read about the lives of those top jockeys, the challenges and the pitfalls they face and how they have made it,' he says. Is there any specific book that highlights the pitfalls of horse racing? 'Not really,' says Paddy, 'but I might write one myself to warn people to stay away from horse racing!'

How did Paddy combine racing with touring abroad? With a laugh, he says that he would 'fit in the tours between the race meetings. That was in America in particular, but also during a few times when I was touring in Australia. On some of our tours down under, I managed to get to the Melbourne Cup race meeting and the Cox Plate, also in Melbourne.'

Paddy still scans the sports pages of the papers to follow who is racing and at what race meetings. He also closely follows the fortunes of his beloved Dublin football and hurling teams.

Another pastime for Paddy in retirement is oil painting. A number of paintings sit on easels in a hallway of his home, some finished and others nearing completion. 'My late wife used to paint, but the difference is that she was good at it. I only do it for occupational therapy, and there is a lady who comes around and gives me some lessons. In fact, I need her to come around again, as I ran into a blind alley with some of them.

'Most of the paintings I do are of country scenes, some that remind me of the rugged beauty of Connemara and some of the lovely landscapes around here. Getting the images into my head is not an easy task, but I keep trying. However, the great masters will never have to worry about any competition from me.'

Paddy is also doing some piano playing during retirement, as it's an instrument that he always thought he would like to be able to play. 'I'm past the stage of the piano and myself being thrown out through the window!' he says. 'It's now a little less daunting than it used to be, and I have moved on a bit with my piano playing. But I think that "progress" would be too elaborate a word to describe where I'm at with it.'

Paddy speaks frankly and freely about what was undoubtedly the biggest battle of his life. While he was in the States, and ironically due to worries about his daughter Ashling, he happened to discover that he had cancer.

'I was in Florida when my daughter rang me, to say that she was very worried and upset about the results of a medical test she had just got. I said that I would go home as quickly as possible. I flew back to New York immediately, where I contacted a friend of mine, Dr Paddy Boland, a very famous bone cancer specialist at Sloan Kettering Hospital in New York City. Paddy is originally from Monasterevin in County Kildare, and has worked at Sloan Kettering for over forty years.

'I said to him that I planned on going back to Ireland and bringing Ashling out to America to see what could be done for her. He replied that I shouldn't do that, but instead he could check out who could be recommended in Ireland, and he would put us in touch with them.'

During the course of the conversation, Paddy, almost by chance, also made arrangements to have himself checked out. 'I had a lot of stomach problems, for two years at that time. Food wasn't staying in my stomach – shortly after I'd eat, I would have to go to the bathroom. To make a long story short, Ashling was negative when all the medical checks were done, but I was positive. Only for her, I would never have found out in time to be saved from cancer.

'The surgeon that operated on me for bowel cancer later became a friend of mine, and told me how lucky I was that it was detected at an early stage. He told me that, of all the cases he was dealing with during that time, only two of the operations that he performed – one on another guy and the one on me – were successful. The cancer was advanced in me, but thankfully not too far advanced.'

Paddy had his surgery in Dublin, and he is loud in his praise of the great work that the doctors, nurses and other medical staff did to restore him to good health. 'It was in St Vincent's Hospital. Professor Des Winter, who performed the operation, is an amazing man, a superhero, who saved my life back then,' he says.

Now, after a lifetime of making a living singing Irish ballads and folk songs on all sorts of stages, Paddy was suddenly on a very different stage, surviving bowel cancer, as his son and daughter anxiously waited and hoped for the best.

He says the most important move for anyone who suspects that they may have cancer is to get it checked as early as possible. 'The longer you let it go, the less chance you have of survival. If you have any suspicion of a growth anywhere in your body, get it checked out immediately. I wouldn't be a person that would visit a doctor regularly, as I thought I was a hardy guy, I thought I was invincible, but nobody is.'

But Paddy says the news that he had cancer wasn't a great blow to him. 'It was no great shock to me, and in fact it was a great relief that it was me and not her – for Christ's sake, she was only twenty-three years old at the time,' he says. 'And sure I had one foot in the grave and another on a banana skin anyway.'

Paddy says he had a positive attitude from the moment he was told he had cancer, and he emphasises the importance of positivity in such a situation. 'Oh my God, being positive is so important, and I had the support of my family as well.'

Ciarán moved home from America, and he and Ashling were hugely supportive of their dad during the toughest battle of his life. 'I had a lot of chemotherapy and radiation treatment. I was fortunate that those treatments didn't make me as sick as they did with other patients. I was going for those treatments with a lot of young women, many of whom sadly didn't survive.

'That was the hardest part for me; they all became my friends. They were all kind, friendly and good-looking young ladies, many only between twenty-five and thirty-five years old. Many of them lost their hair, while I never lost my hair. Obviously, there are different strengths of those treatments that are administered to each person.'

Paddy's chemotherapy and radiation treatments were administered for about three months, to shrink the tumour, before he had surgery. Then, after the operation, there was a year or so for recovery.

He says that he then had no desire to ever go back on the road again. Something that Professor Winter said to him also copper-fastened his thoughts about retiring.

'I was just happy to be back with my family; that was all I really wanted. I was never anxious to go back on the road after that. The professor said to me after I had recovered that the chances of me getting cancer again were almost zero, and if I wanted to go back on stage I could. But then he asked me one further question, and that was, did I find my work on stage very stressful? I was upfront with him, and replied that I was always a very nervous performer. From nine o'clock in the morning when I would get up until I would go on stage that night, I was always nervous – I never got over that down through the years.

'The professor told me that stress is a big contributor to cancer. When he said that, I replied, that's it, I'm finished, I am never going back performing. And I never did,' says Paddy.

Now in retirement, when asked if he would ever take down the banjo and play a tune for his son Ciarán or his sister Jean when they are in his house, Paddy replies, 'Sure they would run away; they wouldn't listen to me! I still have the banjo that I finally got back from Kelly (Luke), having paid a fortune for it when I bought it – my wife would have killed me if she knew what it cost.'

Not alone would Paddy not take down the banjo to play a tune now, he wouldn't even take out one of his own records to play. 'Absolutely not. I could never listen to myself singing anyway, and I wouldn't play them in the car while driving either – sure I'd only crash if I did,' he quips.

However, he says he would sing 'The Fields of Athenry' again if his horse was to win at Cheltenham. 'If he won either the Grand National or the Gold Cup, I'd sing it live then – of course, if he won both races I'd sing it live twice.'

If he is ever to record again, Paddy says that he would make a very different album. It would be one containing songs from the musicals. 'I always admired songs that Richard Tauber did. He was a great lyrical tenor, and I'd love to do some of the songs that he did, such as "Girls Were Made to Love and Kiss". That's a gorgeous song.

'That type of album could contain some songs that my mother would have sung; not necessarily Irish songs. I might do it yet, and if so it will be far removed from anything I've ever done in the past. But I'll have to see if I can scrape up enough money to get into the studio,' he laughs.

That type of album would be very different to what Paddy has been recording all his life. He admits it would be a challenge, but one that he would relish.

'I love operatic material, but never professed to be an opera singer – I never had the timbre in my voice for it. But I loved listening to so many of the great singers. Many great albums were made back in the day, such as

My Fair Lady for example. Nowadays, a Broadway musical usually has only one hit song in it, but every song in *My Fair Lady* was a hit. Not just one, but every song,' he says with conviction.

Reminiscing about his own past achievements in the music business, Paddy says that the success of 'The Fields of Athenry' didn't happen overnight. 'The success of that song kind of crept up on us. While it wasn't an instant hit, it changed my life forever. It meant that I went from playing in small pubs to concert halls and festivals. My life has had its ups and downs, but that was a high, and I didn't have too many disappointments either.'

Among the people Paddy met during his singing career was Pope John Paul II, albeit briefly. 'It was in Trinity College in Washington DC, and there were a lot of invalids there waiting for him to come around. We were entertaining them while they were waiting, and then we entertained the Pope when he arrived.

'A musician friend of mine, a very religious person from Northern Ireland, was with me. He had a child there who was ill, and I took the child up to meet the Pope. He just looked at me, and even though he didn't know if I was a half-believer or a non-believer, he said, "I love you," and I burst out crying – I just lost it,' says Paddy.

The media haven't forgotten Paddy, and apart from regularly referring to him as having sung the definitive version of 'The Fields of Athenry', the newspapers often allude to his other songs as well.

In January 2022, the *Irish Times* included an article about a competition to find a definitive County Monaghan anthem, with a 10,000 Euro prize. The piece referred to Paddy not alone as having recorded a song about Monaghan, but also about all the other thirty-one counties in Ireland.

However, the 'An Irishman's Diary' article, by William Fell, says that neither Paddy nor the great Monaghan poet Patrick Kavanagh included the words 'County Monaghan' in songs that they popularised. 'Unfortunately, the only reference to Monaghan in "Raglan Road" is the "hay" he is no longer making. And that's a bit oblique for an anthem. In any case, Dubliners have already claimed the song as their own.

'Speaking of Dubliners, Paddy Reilly recorded an album some years ago featuring a ballad from each of Ireland's thirty-two counties. Many of his choices were obvious, including "The Curragh of Kildare" and "Limerick You're a Lady". Others were less so, e.g. "Moonlight in Mayo" or, representing Meath, "The Harp That Once".

'But in the case of Monaghan, he was reduced to "The Town of Ballybay", which illustrates our problem well.'

Paddy isn't too concerned about what is written about his songs in the papers. He says the greatest joy of his life now is his great luck in having children and grandchildren visiting him regularly. He was particularly delighted when his daughter Ashling and her husband and son were finally able to visit from the States towards the end of 2021, when some of the COVID-19 restrictions were lifted.

'It was difficult for her to get home up to then and it wasn't possible for me to go to America during that time, as they weren't allowing anyone in while their restrictions were in place. We were really disappointed about not having the graduation ceremony in Harvard. I was sorry for her because she worked so hard to get that Masters. But it was nice that we could have a celebration here in Ireland at Ciarán's house; that was lovely.

'My grandkids are my whole life now. I love them, and I didn't think I'd be that type of person at all. But once they came along, Jez, I got to love all my grandkids. I am so lucky to have a great family – kids and grandkids,' he says.

He is content with his lot in life, and happy to still reside in the village where he was born and grew up. 'The house where I grew up is still standing. It and the two houses beside it in the middle of the village must be the oldest houses there now. Where Ciarán lives now was a site that my father bought, and Diane and I built our house there. My sister Jean and her husband John built the first house there and we built the second one. There has been great progress all around Rathcoole, and it's all changes that are for the better.

'If I had my life to live over again, I wouldn't do anything differently, except maybe being less hard on myself. Life panned out very well for me,' concludes a contented Paddy.

Other books from the O'Brien Press

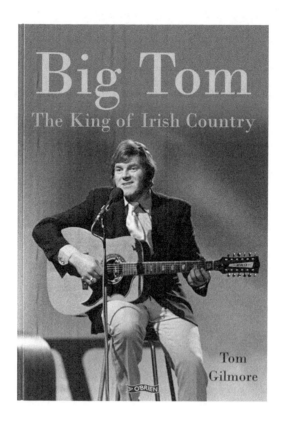

A tribute to Big Tom McBride, 'the Johnny Cash of Irish country music'. From labourer to music star, the journey of the singer who brought so much joy to fans at home and to emigrants abroad over five decades.

Paddy Cole, affectionately known as The King of The Swingers, has taken his style of Jazz, Dixieland and Swing band music all over the world – and back home too. He is the grand old man of Irish Showbiz. Heart-warming and hilarious, this book is full of great stories from the world of music.

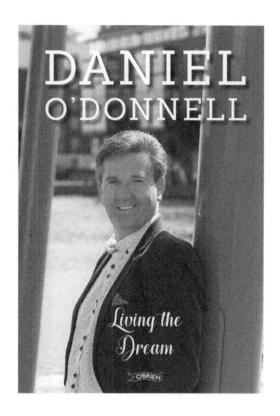

In Ireland, Daniel O'Donnell is more than just a singing star: he has reached the status of 'national treasure'. It has been a long journey for the boy from Kincasslagh, County Donegal, and in *Living the Dream* he tells his story with his customary sense of humour and down-to-earth charm.

Philomena Begley takes us from her happy beginnings as a bread-man's daughter in Pomeroy through the devastating loss of her brother Patsy and the risks of touring Ireland at the height of the Troubles, right up to her fiftieth anniversary in show business in 2012 – her 'gold and silver days'.

The official memoir of Margo O'Donnell, legendary Irish Country Music singer. For fifty years now the name 'Margo' has been synonymous with everything that is positive and enriching in Country and Irish music. This is the story of her life, the successes and difficult times, in her own words.

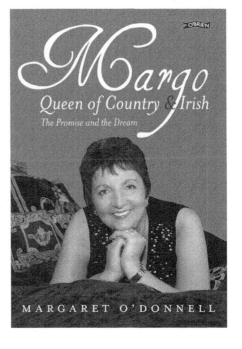